How to control the cost of unemployment compensation claims and taxes on your business

How to control the cost of unemployment compensation claims and taxes on your business

STEWART L. BAILENSON

DJ-I

Dow Jones-Irwin, Inc.
Homewood, Illinois 60430

First Printing, January 1976

ISBN 0-87094-110-0
Library of Congress Catalog Card No. 75–22684

Printed in the United States of America

To Carol, Mark, Ken, Melissa, and Danny—who backed me all the way—but mostly to Carol, who has faithfully supported my every endeavor.

Preface

Somewhere in the cost of your product or service is the cost of unemployment taxes. Reducing (or at least controlling) these taxes, could provide you with the competitive advantage necessary for greater profits.

Companies, as never before, are watching their dollars. Unfortunately, matters pertaining to unemployment compensation are usually handled last and do not receive the attention they deserve.

The words "unemployment compensation" have a great mystique about them. People know that someone who becomes unemployed due to lack of work can collect unemployment compensation benefits. However, there are two areas of misunderstanding regarding unemployment benefits. *Contrary to what many people believe:*

A. Anyone who has worked for an employer covered under the unemployment compensation regulations can collect unemployment benefits. The reason for separation does not make any difference. A person could have been laid off because of lack of work, discharged for misconduct, or could have voluntarily quit, and will be able to collect unemployment benefits. There might be a slight delay in the receipt of benefits, however, eventually that person should receive benefits.

B. The employer, in one way or another, usually bears the cost of unemployment benefits. Except for recent emergency legislation covering these emergency benefits only, the federal government does not pay. Neither do the funds for unemployment benefits come from the employee himself, through deductions in his wages.

When the unemployment regulations were originally passed in the 1930s, the intent was to help the individual out of work through no fault of his own. Through changes in these regulations over the years, even a person who quits or is discharged for misconduct can collect these benefits. The employer bears the cost of unemployment compensation through an unemployment tax that is paid to each state in which the employer pays wages. The tax rate itself is a certain percentage of that employer's taxable payroll (i.e., varies from state to state) and this tax, usually applicable for a calendar year, is determined annually and is based on certain experience factors—those being taxable payroll, prior contributions, and unemployment benefits drawn by former employees that were charged to the employer.

The unemployment tax is a very expensive burden for a company. The tax comes "off the top" and, therefore, cannot be used to produce income. It is a payroll overhead, as is Social

Security. *However, there is one large difference —the Social Security tax rate is fixed by law.* The Social Security rate an employer pays does not vary according to the employer's experience. *The unemployment tax rate does vary according to the employer's experience.* If there have not been many charges to the employer when former employees collect unemployment benefits, his tax rate will generally be low (in some states, as low as "0"); if a significant number of former employees have drawn benefits charged to the employer, his tax rate will generally be high (as high as 6.6% in Michigan).

As an example of tax dollars involved, suppose an employer employs 100 people and the taxable wage base is $5,000 for each employee. Suppose further that the minimum tax rate is 0% and the maximum tax rate is 3.6%:

100 employees, times $5,000 per person = $500,000 total taxable wages.

If the employer's tax rate is 0%, he pays nothing to the state. However, if his tax rate is the maximum of 3.6%, he would pay $18,000 to the state. There is no return on this money. Once it is paid, it is lost. The money is paid as a tax, so it can't produce income. A company operating on a 2% margin would have to generate tens of thousands of dollars to produce the $18,000 for unemployment taxes.

Just think—in the example cited above, the company that pays out only $18,000 a year in unemployment taxes, pays $180,000 in ten years

—and this money is paid to former employees who produce nothing for the company.

Through the procedures discussed in this book, obtained in over ten years of experience, substantial sums of money can be saved through lower tax rates. Through the effective control of changes in corporate structure, personnel policies, disposition of unemployment claim forms and benefit charges, and by realizing that unemployment compensation taxes are controllable, lower tax rates should result.

We will talk mainly of preventive maintenance. By knowing what to do and how to do it, the end result will be predictable.

This book was not intended to be voluminous. The author will not derive satisfaction from the number of words he has written, but from the content and the help employers should receive. Any reference to companies or people is purely coincidental.

Contrary to some thinking, the various state unemployment agencies will provide whatever help they can to answer questions and keep the employer informed on changes in unemployment regulations. There are also several companies that will, for a fee, provide all of the services described in this handbook. Whether or not you employ such a service, this handbook can be a useful asset in controlling and reducing your unemployment tax payments.

December 1975

STEWART L. BAILENSON

Contents

List of exhibits

chapter 1

State tax payments

Each employer covered under state unemployment regulations must submit a quarterly contribution (wage) report. Normally, this report must be submitted on or before the last day of the month following each quarter. Failure to pay state unemployment taxes on time can result in the following costly penalties:

1. The state may not give you credit for the contributions and/or the taxable payroll amount, thereby causing a substantial increase in your tax rate for the following year.
2. You may not receive the full 2.7 percent credit on your federal unemployment tax payments. Normally, when paying your annual federal unemployment taxes, you can deduct 2.7 percent for the state unemployment taxes paid on time. However, failure to pay your state unemployment taxes on time can result in this credit being reduced by 10 percent. For example:

All credits received:

Federal taxable payroll	$500,000
	3.2%
	$ 16,000
Less: 2.7% credit	13,500
Federal unemployment tax (0.5%)	$ 2,500

Late payments—reduced credit:

Federal taxable payroll	$500,000
	3.2%
	$ 16,000
Less: 2.7% credit	13,500
Federal unemployment tax (0.5%)	$ 2,500
Plus 10% penalty	250
Total payment due	$ 2,750

CAUTION. In states of Kansas and Michigan, quarterly wage reports must be submitted no later than the 25th day of the month following the end of the quarter.

Unemployment compensation tax base

The tax base is the amount of earnings for each employee on which unemployment taxes are paid. Each state determines its own tax base. Depending on the state, tax bases vary from $4,200 per person to $10,000 per person. Of course, as unemployment benefits increase, the tax bases must also increase so that funds will be available to pay for these benefits.

An employer in California (tax base, $4,200 per person) that employed 500 people would have a total taxable payroll of $2,100,000, computed as follows:

Taxable payroll per employee	$	4,200
Number of employees		× 500
		$2,100,000

Tax rate and payment

The California employer who has a taxable payroll of $2,100,000 would have a tax rate of from 1.7 percent to 4.1 percent. Suppose this employer's tax rate was 3.0 percent. As an example of how this tax would be paid over the four calendar quarters, consider the following:

	First quarter	*Second quarter*	*Third quarter*	*Fourth quarter*	*Totals*
Gross payroll.......	$900,000	$900,000	$900,000	$900,000	$3,600,000
Excess payroll (over $4,200).....	100,000	300,000	500,000	600,000	1,500,000
Taxable payroll.....	800,000	600,000	400,000	300,000	2,100,000
Tax rate...........	3.0%	3.0%	3.0%	3.0%	3.0%
Contribution amount..........	$ 24,000	$ 18,000	$ 12,000	$ 9,000	$ 63,000

These payments are spread over the calendar year; however, as can be seen from this example, about 40 percent of the annual tax payments are normally paid during the first quarter of the calendar year. This is because few employees would have earned the tax base of $4,200 by March 31. This can be important to remember when budgeting.

CAUTION. If you have employees in Iowa, your tax rate cannot be higher than 2.7 percent on the first $10,000 of taxable wages *each quarter*. For example, suppose your taxable payroll the first quarter was $100,000 and your tax rate was 3.0 percent—

		Total Payment
$10,000	$90,000	
2.7%	3.0%	
$ 270	$ 2,700	$2,970

If you have employees in Illinois, your tax rate cannot be higher than 2.7 percent on the first $20,000 of taxable wages *each quarter*. Therefore, don't inadvertently pay too much to these states if your tax rate is higher than 2.7 percent.

Transferring employees from one state to another

If you transfer employees from one state to another within the same corporation, there is no need to start over on the tax base in the state in which they were transferred. When determining if any taxes should be paid for the transferred individual, take into account what his or her wages were from January 1 until the date of the transfer. For example, suppose someone earns $3,700 in Iowa from January 1, 1975 until June 1, 1975, and is then transferred to California and earns $5,000 from June 1, 1975 to December 31, 1975. Suppose the tax base in both states is $5,000 per person. After the employee moves, the only wages on which taxes should be paid is $1,300.

Tax base	$5,000
Earnings in Iowa	3,700
Remaining taxable wages	$1,300

CAUTION. If an employee is transferred into Kentucky, Nevada, or Utah, you cannot take advantage of the wages you previously paid this employee. You must start over.

CAUTION. The tax saving described above applies only if an employee, when transferred, remains with the same corporation. If the employee starts working for another corporation after being transferred, this corporation must start over on the employee's wage base.

Experience rating

All state regulations have in effect some system of experience rating by which individual employers' contribution rates are varied from the standard rate on the basis of their experience.[1] It is a system used by the states under which the unemployment tax of each individual employer is determined on the basis of the employer's experience. For example, if an employer's benefit charges for the preceding fiscal year have increased from the previous year, normally his or her unemployment tax rate will increase. Employers with more stable employment are usually assigned the lower rates. However, even though an employer may have stable employment, if no effort is made to implement any control procedures, the employer's tax rate may be too high. Because of the complexities of the unemployment regulations, many employers are not aware of the procedures that should be followed to reduce their tax rate.

Without individual employer experience rating, there would disappear from the unemployment compensation program the basic financial interest for employers to stabilize their employment. If unemployment benefits were to be financed by a flat rate payroll tax, the same for all employers regardless of the individual employer's experience, employers would have no greater interest in unemployment compensation administration than they now have in the administration of the social security program, which is financed by a flat rate payroll tax. Also without individual employer experience rating, the purpose for which unemployment compensa-

---

[1] "Experience" normally refers to any or all of the following: (1) contributions paid, (2) benefit charges, (3) account balance, and (4) taxable payroll.

tion was designed would eventually be lost to a relief program.

Rates under experience rating

The standard rate of contribution under many state unemployment compensation regulations is 2.7 percent. Generally, the standard rate applies to employers who are not subject to the experience-rating provisions because they have not had employment for a long enough period of time. However, the standard rate may also apply to employers who are subject to such provisions but who are not entitled to a different rate because of their experience-rating record. Experience rates may be much higher or much lower than standard rates. In some states the standard rate, or the maximum rate, also applies to employers who failed to file reports or pay contributions on time.

Ordinarily, employers subject to an experience-rating system are entitled to a reduced rate if they have had a favorable experience-rating record. If their record is unfavorable, they must contribute at the standard rate, or they may have to contribute at a higher rate if the state regulation so provides. The maximum rate in the majority of states is now higher than 2.7 percent, and the number of states with a maximum rate of higher than 2.7 percent increases steadily.

As will be shown, the way in which employer rates are varied from the standard rate differs from state to state. The amount in the state fund is naturally an important factor to be considered in fixing contribution rates. Unemployment benefits are paid out of contributions collected by the state and, consequently, contribution rates must ultimately be increased when the amount available for the payment of benefits is substantially reduced by increases in benefit payments. The various experience-rating systems provide for increasing rates when this occurs. Under normal conditions, the balance in a fund can be restored to a safe level by a general increase in contribution rates, but the fact remains that a severe period of unemployment can mean a severe reduction in taxable payrolls. This, in turn, tends to counteract an increase in contribution rates. Therefore, large balances in state funds are necessary, which is the reason that many states do not permit contribution rates of less than 2.7 percent unless the fund has a balance of a specified amount. Some states protect the solvency of the fund by allowing reduced rates only if the balance of the fund equals a certain percentage of the total taxable wages paid by all employers during the preceding year. Other states require that the fund balance equal or exceed the amount of benefits paid in some preceding period. More than one schedule of rates are provided in most states, with the balance in the fund being the determining factor as to which of the schedules shall apply.

Even though, as mentioned elsewhere, the general experience of all employers in the state will have an effect on all tax rates, that is, higher or lower tax rate schedules, the experience of the individual employer will be the final determinant of the employer's own rate. In order to control and reduce your tax rate, you must control the benefit charges through the procedures to be discussed. Generally speaking, if your benefit charges increase, your tax rate will increase.

Types of experience-rating formulas

As explained elsewhere, all states have some system of experience rating by which individual employers' contribution rates can be varied on the basis of their experience. The experience-rating provisions of state regulations vary greatly. The most significant variations grow out of differences in the formulas used for rate determinations. The factor used to measure experience with unemployment is the basic variable which makes it possible to establish the relative incidence of unemployment among the workers of different employers. Differences in such experience represent the major justification for differences in tax rates, either to provide an incentive for stabilization of unemployment or to allocate the cost of unemployment.

At present there are four distinct taxation systems, usually identified as reserve ratio, benefit ratio, benefit-wage ratio, and payroll-variation formulas. A few states have combinations of the systems. In spite of significant differences, all systems have certain common characteristics. All formulas are devised to establish the relative experience of individual employers with unemployment or with benefit costs. To this end, all have factors for measuring each employer's experience with unemployment or benefit expenditures, and all compare this experience with a measure of exposure—usually payrolls—to establish the relative experience of large and small employers. However, the four systems differ greatly in the construction of the formulas, in the factors used to measure experience and the methods of measurement, in the number of years over which the experience is recorded, in the presence or absence of other factors, and in the relative weight given the various factors in the final assignment of rates. The factor used to measure experience with unemployment is the heart of the rating system. It is the basic variable which makes it possible to establish the relative incidence of unemployment among the workers of different employers. Differences in such experience represent the major justification for differences in tax rates, whether the purpose is to provide an incentive for stabilization of employment or to allocate the costs of unemployment. As a guide to the relative risk of unemployment among employers, each individual employer's unemployment record is compared with the employer's payroll.

Here, however, any similarity in the various systems ends. They differ in the construction of the formulas, in the factors used to measure experience and the methods of measurement, in the number of years over which the experience is recorded, in the presence or absence of other factors, and in the relative weight given to the various factors in the final assignment of rates. See Exhibit 1–1 for a listing of the experience-rating plans adopted by each state.

Reserve ratio formula. The reserve ratio was the earliest of the experience-rating formulas and continues to be the most popular. The sys-

EXHIBIT 1–1

Types of experience rating

State	Type	State	Type
Ala.	Benefit-wage ratio	N.C.	Reserve ratio
Alaska	Payroll variation	N.D.	Reserve ratio
Ariz.	Reserve ratio	Neb.	Reserve ratio
Ark.	Reserve ratio	Nev.	Reserve ratio
Calif.	Reserve ratio	N.H.	Reserve ratio
Colo.	Reserve ratio	N.J.	Reserve ratio
Conn.	Benefit ratio	N.M.	Reserve ratio
D.C.	Reserve ratio	N.Y.	Reserve ratio
Del.	Benefit-wage ratio	Ohio	Reserve ratio
Fla.	Benefit ratio	Okla.	Benefit-wage ratio
Ga.	Reserve ratio	Ore.	Benefit ratio
Hawaii	Reserve ratio	Pa.	Benefit ratio and reserve ratio
Id.	Payroll variation and reserve ratio	P.R.	None
Ill.	Benefit-wage ratio	R.I.	Reserve ratio
Ind.	Reserve ratio	S.C.	Reserve ratio
Iowa	Reserve ratio	S.D.	Reserve ratio
Kans.	Reserve ratio	Tenn.	Reserve ratio
Ky.	Reserve ratio	Tex.	Benefit ratio
La.	Reserve ratio	Utah	Payroll variation
Mass.	Reserve ratio	Vt.	Benefit ratio
Me.	Reserve ratio	Va.	Benefit-wage ratio
Md.	Benefit ratio	Wash.	Payroll variation and benefit ratio
Mich.	Reserve ratio		
Minn.	Benefit ratio	W. Va.	Reserve ratio
Miss.	Benefit ratio	Wis.	Reserve ratio
Mo.	Reserve ratio	Wyo.	Benefit ratio
Mont.	Payroll variation and benefit ratio		

tem is essentially cost accounting. On each employer's record are entered the amount of the employer's payroll, the employer's contributions, and the benefits paid to employees. The benefits are subtracted from the contributions, and the resulting balance is divided by the payroll to determine the size of the balance in terms of the potential liability for benefits inherent in wage payments. The balance carried forward each year under the reserve ratio plan is ordinarily the difference between the employer's total contributions and the total benefits received by the employer's workers since the employer became liable under the law.

$$\text{Reserve ratio} = \frac{\text{Contributions} - \text{Benefit charges}}{\text{Taxable payroll}}$$

About two thirds of the states listed below allow employers to make extra tax payments—"voluntary contributions"—to secure a lower rate. A reserve account does not stop when business is discontinued. When an employer stops doing business in a reserve ratio state, the employer's reserve account is not immediately lost (unless the employer applies for termination of coverage); the account stays on the books either indefinitely or for a specific length of time. If the employer resumes operation in the state before the account is closed out, the past record of taxes and benefit charges of the employer counts in determining any future merit rate.

Before an employer's rate is reduced, a specified reserve must be accumulated and maintained; then rates are assigned according to a schedule of rates for specified ranges of reserve ratio—again, the higher the ratio, the lower the rate. This formula is designed to make sure that no employer will be granted a rating reduction unless over the years more is contributed to the fund than drawn in benefits.

The 32 states using the reserve ratio formula are as follows:

Arizona, VC[2]	Missouri, VC
Arkansas, VC	Nebraska, VC
California	Nevada
Colorado, VC	New Hampshire
D.C., VC	New Jersey, VC
Georgia	New Mexico, VC
Hawaii	New York, VC
Idaho	North Carolina, VC
Indiana, VC	North Dakota, VC
Iowa, VC	Ohio, VC
Kansas, VC	Rhode Island
Kentucky, VC	South Carolina, VC
Louisiana, VC	South Dakota, VC
Maine, VC	Tennessee
Massachusetts	West Virginia, VC
Michigan, VC	Wisconsin, VC

Reserve ratio relationships

Taxable payroll ↑ Benefit charges ↑ = Tax rate increase
Taxable payroll ↑ Benefit charges ↓ = Rate increase*
Taxable payroll ↑ Benefit charges— = Tax rate increase
Taxable payroll—Benefit charges ↑ = Tax rate increase
Taxable payroll—Benefit charges ↓ = Tax rate decrease
Taxable payroll—Benefit charges— = No change in tax rate
Taxable payroll ↓ Benefit charges ↑ = Tax rate decrease†
Taxable payroll ↓ Benefit charges ↓ = Tax rate decrease
Taxable payroll ↓ Benefit charges— = Tax rate decrease

* Unless benefit charges decrease enough to cancel the effect of an increase in taxable payroll.

† Unless benefit charges increase enough to cancel the effect of a decrease in taxable payroll.

Rates depend both on how many workers become unemployed and how long they draw benefits.

Rates are based on long-term experience. Each year's rate depends on the employer's history of taxes and benefits. When a busi-

---

[2] VC indicates that a voluntary contribution can be made to reduce the tax rate (see section in this chapter entitled "Voluntary Contribution").

ness changes hands, the reserve account may go with it.

The two most important relationships to remember are:

1. As taxable payroll increases, the unemployment tax rate increases (assuming benefit charges remain approximately equal from one year to the next).[3]
2. As benefit charges decrease, the unemployment tax rate decreases (assuming taxable payroll does not significantly change from one year to the next).[4]

It would follow, then, that in order to decrease your unemployment tax rate, either decrease your taxable payroll and/or decrease your benefit charges. Of course, your taxable payroll cannot be decreased at will. However, your benefit charges can be *controlled* through effective personnel and tax control procedures.

See Exhibit 1–2 for an example of a reserve ratio tax rate computation.

Benefit ratio formula. The benefit ratio formula also uses benefits as the measure of experience, but it eliminates contributions from the formula and relates benefits directly to payrolls. The index for rate variation is the ratio of benefits to payrolls. The theory is that if each employer pays a rate that approximates the employer's benefit ratio, the program will be ad-

---

[3] Of course, the converse would be true, that is, as taxable payroll decreases, the tax rate decreases (benefit charges remaining equal).

[4] The converse of this would also be true.

EXHIBIT 1–2

Example of reserve ratio tax rate computation for the year beginning January 1, 1976

Account balance, 6/30/74		$ 8,900
Add: Contributions, 7/1/74–6/30/75		1,800
Total		$ 10,700
Less: Benefit charges, 7/1/74–6/30/75		50
Account balance, 6/30/75		$ 10,650
Taxable payrolls:		
7/1/72–6/30/73	$125,000	
7/1/73–6/30/74	160,000	
7/1/74–6/30/75	176,700	
Total	$461,700	
Average annual payroll, 7/1/72–6/30/75	$\frac{\$461,700}{3}$ =	$153,900
Reserve ratio, $\frac{\$10,650}{\$153,900}$		6.92%
Contribution rate		1.2%

Contribution rate table—reserve ratio

Reserve ratio (percent)	*Tax rate (percent)*
0– 3.0	2.0
3.0– 4.0	1.8
4.0– 5.0	1.6
5.0– 6.0	1.4
6.0– 7.0	1.2
7.0– 8.0	1.0
8.0– 9.0	0.8
9.0–10.0	0.6
10.0–11.0	0.4
11.0–12.0	0.2
12.0–13.0	0.1
Over 13.0	0.0

Note: It can be seen here that the higher the reserve ratio, the lower the contribution rate.

equately financed. In some of the states in which this type of program is used, rates are further varied by the inclusion of three or more schedules, effective at specified levels of the amount in the state fund, either in terms of dollar amounts or a proportion of payrolls. Other factors may also be considered.

The benefit ratio system is geared to short-term experience. Only the benefits paid in the most recent three years are used. Adjustment for newly subject employers is automatic under this formula because benefits paid in the most recent one or two years are related to payrolls for the same period.

$$\text{Benefit ratio} = \frac{\text{Benefit charges}}{\text{Taxable payroll}}$$

Rates depend both on how many workers become unemployed and how long they draw benefits.

Rates depend on short-term experience. A good year or a bad one cannot affect a ratio for more than three years.

The ten states using the benefit ratio formula are as follows:

Connecticut	Oregon
Florida	Pennsylvania
Maryland	Texas
Minnesota	Vermont
Mississippi	Wyoming

The states of Pennsylvania, Minnesota, and Wyoming allow employers to make "voluntary contributions" to secure a lower tax rate. (See section in this chapter entitled "Voluntary Contributions.")

Benefit ratio relationships

Taxable payroll ↑ Benefit charges ↑ = Tax rate decrease*
Taxable payroll ↑ Benefit charges ↓ = Tax rate decrease
Taxable payroll ↑ Benefit charges— = Tax rate decrease
Taxable payroll—Benefit charges ↑ = Tax rate increase
Taxable payroll—Benefit charges ↓ = Tax rate decrease
Taxable payroll—Benefit charges— = No change in tax rate
Taxable payroll ↓ Benefit charges ↑ = Tax rate increase
Taxable payroll ↓ Benefit charges ↓ = Tax rate increase†
Taxable payroll ↓ Benefit charges— = Tax rate increase

* Unless benefit charges increase enough to cancel the effect of an increase in taxable payroll.

† Unless benefit charges decrease enough to cancel the effect of a decrease in taxable payroll.

The two most important relationships to remember are:

1. As taxable payroll increases, the unemployment tax rate decreases (assuming benefit charges remain approximately equal from one year to the next).[5]
2. As benefit charges decrease, the unemployment tax rate decreases (assuming taxable payroll does not significantly change from one year to the next).[6]

It would follow, then, that in order to decrease your unemployment tax rate, either increase your taxable payroll and/or decrease your benefit charges.

---

[5] The converse would also be true, that is, as taxable payroll decreases, the tax rate increases (benefit charges remaining equal).

[6] The converse of this would also be true.

In an expanding economy, as employers add employees to their payroll, tax rates would decrease (if benefit charges did not increase). However, this would be more of an uncontrollable cause and effect relationship rather than the result of an attempt to decrease your unemployment tax rate. As the need for your product or service increases, you will likewise increase the number of production and office employees. Therefore, the one controllable factor is your benefit charges. Your benefit charges can be *controlled* through effective personnel and tax procedures. These relationships are identical to those of the benefit-wage ratio, discussed below, although their formulas are different. See Exhibit 1–3 for an example of a benefit-ratio tax rate computation.

Benefit-wage ratio formula. The benefit-wage ratio formula is radically different. It makes no attempt to measure all benefits paid to the workers of individual employers. The relative experience of employers is measured by separations of workers that result in benefit payments, but the duration of their benefits is not a factor. The separations, weighted with the wages earned by the workers with each base-period employer, are recorded on each employer's experience-rating record as "benefit wages." Only one separation per beneficiary per benefit year is recorded for any one employer, but the charging of any benefit wages is postponed until a prescribed amount of benefits has been paid: for example, in Alabama and Oklahoma, until payment is made for the second week of unemploy-

EXHIBIT 1–3

Example of tax benefit ratio rate computation for the year beginning January 1, 1976

Benefit charges:		
1973	$ 800	
1974	700	
1975	1,450	
Total		$ 2,950
Taxable payroll:		
1973	$150,000	
1974	200,000	
1975	193,000	
		$543,000
Benefit ratio	$\frac{\$\ 2{,}950}{\$543{,}000} =$	0.0054%
Contribution rate		2.6%

Contribution rate table—benefit ratio

Range of benefit ratios (percent)	*Tax rates (percent)*
0.00000–0.00000	1.1
0.00001–0.00024	1.4
0.00025–0.00115	1.7
0.00116–0.00233	2.0
0.00234–0.00423	2.3
0.00424–0.00561	2.6
0.00562–0.00763	2.9
0.00764–0.01172	3.2
0.01173–0.02119	3.5
0.02120–0.03851	3.8
0.03852–infinity	4.1

Note: It can be seen here that the higher the benefit ratio, the higher the contribution rate.

ment; in Illinois and Virginia, until the benefits paid equal three times the weekly benefit amount; and in Delaware, as soon as benefits are paid. The index which is used to establish the relative experience of employers is the proportion of each employer's payroll which is paid to those workers of the employer who become unemployed and receive benefits, that is, the employer's "benefit wages" to total taxable wages.

As under the benefit ratio formula, adjustment for newly subject employers is automatic under the benefit-wage ratio formula. The ratio of an employer's "benefit wages" to total taxable payroll can be computed for one, two, or three years.

$$\text{Benefit-wage ratio} = \frac{\text{Benefit wages}}{\text{Taxable payroll}}$$

The formula is designed to assess variable rates that will raise the equivalent of the total amount paid out as benefits. The percentage relationship between total benefit payments and total benefit wages in the state during three years is determined. This ratio, known as the "state experience factor," means that, on the average, the workers who drew benefits received a certain amount of benefits for each dollar of benefit wages paid and the same amount of taxes per dollar of benefit wages is needed to replenish the fund. The total amount to be raised is distributed among employers in accordance with their benefit-wage ratios; the higher the ratio, the higher the rate.

Individual employers' rates are determined by multiplying the employer's experience factor by the state experience factor. The multiplication is facilitated by a table that assigns rates the same as, or slightly more than, the product of the employer's benefit-wage ratio and the state factor. The range of the rates is, however, limited by a minimum and maximum. The minimum and the rounding upward of some rates tend to increase the amount that would be raised if the plan were effected without the table; the maximum, however, decreases the income from employers who would otherwise have paid higher rates.

The five states using the benefit-wage ratio formula are:

Alabama	Oklahoma
Delaware	Virginia
Illinois	

As mentioned above, the index which is used to establish the relative experience of employers is the ratio of the employer's benefit wages to total taxable wages. If employer A has a $100,000 payroll and employer B has a $75,000 payroll, and each pays $25,000 to workers who later become unemployed and receive compensation, their state experience factors are as follows:

A's experience factor would be $\frac{25{,}000}{100{,}000}$
or 25 percent

B's experience factor would be $\frac{25{,}000}{75{,}000}$
or 33.3 percent

The next step is to determine the percentage relationship between total benefit payments and total benefit wages in the state during a specified number of years.

If benefits during this period were 2 million and total benefit wages 25 million, the ratio or *state* experience factor is 2,000,000/25,000,000 or 8 percent.

The final step, then, in determining the individual employer's rate involves multiplying the employer's experience factor by the state experience factor.

Employer A.	25% × 8 = 2.0%
Employer B.	33.3% × 8 = 2.6%

Rates depend on how many workers become unemployed, but not on how long they draw benefits. Only one charge is made for each worker, and it is made sometime in the worker's first three weeks of benefits. Rates are based on short-term experience, and a good year or a bad one cannot effect the rate for longer than three years. A payroll *increase* tends to lower the rate, and a *decrease* tends to raise it.

Benefit-wage ratio relationships

Taxable payroll ↑	Benefit charges ↑	=	Tax rate decrease*
Taxable payroll ↑	Benefit charges ↓	=	Tax rate decrease
Taxable payroll ↑	Benefit charges—	=	Tax rate decrease
Taxable payroll—	Benefit charges ↑	=	Tax rate increase
Taxable payroll—	Benefit charges ↓	=	Tax rate decrease
Taxable payroll—	Benefit charges—	=	No change in tax rate
Taxable payroll ↓	Benefit charges ↑	=	Tax rate increase
Taxable payroll ↓	Benefit charges ↓	=	Tax rate increase†
Taxable payroll ↓	Benefit charges—	=	Tax rate increase

* Unless benefit charges increase enough to cancel the effect of an increase in taxable payroll.

† Unless benefit charges decrease enough to cancel the effect of a decrease in taxable payroll.

These relationships are identical to those of the benefit ratio, discussed above. Here again the two most important relationships to remember are:

1. As taxable payroll increases, the unemployment tax rate decreases (assuming benefit charges remain approximately equal from one year to the next).[7]
2. As benefit charges decrease, the unemployment tax rate decreases (assuming taxable payroll does not significantly change from one year to the next).[8]

It would follow, then, that in order to decrease your unemployment tax rate, either increase your taxable payroll and/or decrease your benefit charges.

In an expanding economy, as employers add employees to their payroll, tax rates would decrease (if benefit charges did not increase). However, this would be more of an uncontrollable cause and effect relationship rather than the result of an attempt to decrease your unemployment tax rate. As the need for your product or service increases, you will likewise increase your production and office employees. Therefore, the one controllable factor is your benefit charges. Your benefit charges can be *controlled* through effective personnel and tax procedures. See Exhibit 1–4 for an example of a benefit-wage ratio tax rate computation.

Payroll-variation formula. The payroll-variation plan, used separately or in combination with other factors, is independent of benefit payments to individual workers; neither benefits

[7] The converse would also be true, that is, as taxable payroll decreases, the tax rate increases (benefit charges remaining equal).

[8] The converse of this would also be true.

nor any benefit derivatives are used to measure unemployment. An employer's experience with unemployment is measured by the decline in the employer's payrolls from year to year or from quarter to quarter. The declines are expressed as a percentage of payrolls so that experience of employers with large and small payrolls may be compared. If an employer's payroll shows no decrease, or only a small percentage decrease over a given period, the employer will be eligible for the largest proportional reductions. This use of payroll declines as a measure of unemployment risk is based on the assumption that the hazard of unemployment exists if an employer is unable to offer as much employment in one period as was offered in the immediately preceding period. These plans use annual and/or quarterly declines in total payrolls (not total taxable payrolls) as the measure of each em-

EXHIBIT 1–4

Example of tax benefit-wage ratio rate computation for the year beginning January 1, 1976

Benefit wages:		
7/1/72–6/30/73	$ 150,000	
7/1/73–6/30/74	200,000	
7/1/74–6/30/75	40,000	
Total		$ 390,000
Taxable payroll:		
7/1/72–6/30/73	$ 3,500,000	
7/1/73–6/30/74	3,700,000	
7/1/74–6/30/75	4,100,000	
Total		$11,300,000
Benefit-wage ratio	$\frac{\$\ 390{,}000}{\$11{,}300{,}000} =$	3.45%
Contribution rate		0.3%

EXHIBIT 1–4 (*continued*)

Contribution rate table—benefit-wage ratio

Benefit-wage ratio (percent)	*Tax rate (percent)*
0 to less than 1.665	0.1
1.665 to less than 2.775	0.2
2.775 to less than 3.885	0.3
3.885 to less than 5.000	0.4
5.000 to less than 7.225	0.5
7.225 to less than 8.335	0.6
8.335 to less than 9.445	0.7
9.445 to less than 10.555	0.8
10.555 to less than 11.665	0.9
11.665 to less than 12.775	1.0
12.775 to less than 13.885	1.1
13.885 to less than 15.000	1.2
15.000 to less than 16.115	1.3
16.115 to less than 17.225	1.4
17.225 to less than 18.335	1.5
18.335 to less than 19.445	1.6
19.445 to less than 20.555	1.7
20.555 to less than 21.665	1.8
21.665 to less than 22.775	1.9
22.775 to less than 23.885	2.0
23.885 to less than 25.000	2.1
25.000 to less than 26.115	2.2
26.115 to less than 27.225	2.3
27.225 to less than 28.335	2.4
28.335 to less than 29.445	2.5
29.445 to less than 30.555	2.6
30.555 and over	2.7

ployer's experience with unemployment and adjust the amount of revenue that is to be raised in any year to the needs of the program as measured by current reserves. Each employer's rate is based on the employer's experience with declines in payroll, from year to year and from quarter to quarter. The extent of each decline is reduced to a percentage basis. If the payroll for the quarter ending on September 30 was $100,000 and the payroll for the quarter ending on December 31 was $90,000, the percentage decline would be 10 percent. The average of an employer's percentage declines during the experience period is the experience index which establishes the relative experience of one employer as compared with other employers during the same period.

The payroll-variation system is used in only four states:

Alaska	Utah
Montana	Washington

Montana has a system which is a combination of the benefit ratio and payroll variation. There is actually no consistency of system among these states.

Alaska measures the stability of payrolls from quarter to quarter over a three-year period.

Washington measures the last three years' annual payrolls on a theory that over a period of time the greatest drains on the fund result from the decline in general business activity.

Utah measures the stability of both annual and quarterly payroll and a third factor, the duration of liability of contributions commonly called the age factor. This particular plan has the advantage of administrative simplicity. Few procedures are necessary. The records are on file, and the machinery for contribution collection should assure the accuracy of the figures.

There is no need for a procedure for charging benefits paid—no need for notices to employers on charges or procedure for appealing charges.

In these states, employee turnover will not necessarily raise the rate if a replacement is soon hired at the same wage level. Rates are based on short-term experience—usually from three to five years.

A payroll decrease raises the rate in all of these states. Another decided advantage of the plan is that it eliminates the close relationship which exists under most experience-rating systems between each benefit payment and some employer's rate.

This basis of measurement possesses certain disadvantages, however. It takes no account of turnover. An employer's payroll might remain constant even with a high rate of turnover. Overtime, as well as part-time work, would count against an employer. For example, an employer might operate overtime one month and at a normal schedule the next month, with a consequent decline in payroll. Moreover, payroll fluctuations give no weight to duration of unemployment. A layoff of one month would have the same effect as a layoff for three months. Finally, payroll fluctuations are heavily influenced by factors extraneous to employment, such as changes in wage rates, payment of bonuses, the occurrence of holidays, and so forth. Some states have recognized this disadvantage by allowing employers, upon request, to apportion bonuses and lump-sum payments. See Exhibit 1–5 for an example of a payroll-variation tax rate computation.

EXHIBIT 1–5

Example of payroll-variation tax rate computation for the year beginning January 1, 1976

Calendar year	*Quarter*	*Total wages*	*Quarterly decline (percent)*	*Calendar year total wages*	*Annual decline (percent)*
1973	1st	$300,000			
	2d	400,000			
	3d	350,000	12.50		
	4th	400,000		$1,450,000	
1974	1st	315,000	21.25		
	2d	340,000			
	3d	250,000	26.47		
	4th	310,000		1,215,000	16.21
1975	1st	250,000	19.35		
	2d	300,000			
	3d	275,000	8.33		
	4th	250,000	9.09	1,075,000	11.52
Total			96.99		27.73

	Sum	*Factor*
Quarterly decline (quarterly factor)	96.99	6
Year's contribution liability (age factor)	20	5
Annual decline (calendar year factor)	27.73	4
Total (experience factor)		15
Class	6	
State reserve ratio rate	1.8%	

The objective in the example is to determine to which "class" the employer belongs. The sum of the following determines to which "class" the employer belongs:

1. The *quarterly factor* is computed by adding up the quarterly decrease percentages in total wages, if any, for each of the quarters in the three calendar years in the experience period—that is, the three years immediately preceding the year for which rates are being determined. The decrease percentage for any quarter in the experience period is determined by dividing any decrease in total wages in this quarter from the preceding quarter by the total wages of the *earlier* of these two quarters, the division being carried to the fourth decimal place and any remaining fraction disregarded. After the quarterly decrease percentages for the quarters in the experi-

EXHIBIT 1–5 (*continued*)

ence period have been added together, the quarterly factor is determined from the following table:

Sum of quarterly decrease percentages	*Quarterly factor*
Less than 40%	12
40% or more but less than 50%	11
50% or more but less than 60%	10
60% or more but less than 70%	9
70% or more but less than 80%	8
80% or more but less than 90%	7
90% or more but less than 100%	6
100% or more but less than 120%	5
120% or more but less than 150%	4
150% or more but less than 200%	3
200% or more but less than 250%	2
250% or more but less than 300%	1
300% or more	0

2. The *age factor* is determined, in accordance with the following table, on the basis of full consecutive calendar years of contribution liability preceding the year for which rates are being determined:

Years of liability for contributions	*Age factor*
8 years or more	5
4 years or more but less than 8 years	4
Less than 4 years	3

3. The *calendar year factor* is computed by adding up the calendar year decrease percentages in total wages, if any, for each of the three calendar years in the experience period—that is, the three years immediately preceding the year for which rates are being determined. The decrease percentage for any year in the experience period is determined by dividing any decrease in total wages in this year from the preceding year by the total wages of the *earlier*

EXHIBIT 1–5 (*continued*)

of these two years, the division being carried to the fourth decimal place and any remaining fraction disregarded. "Total wages" means all remuneration paid by an employer to employees for insured work. After the calendar year decrease percentages for the years in the experience period have been added together, the calendar year factor is determined from the following table:

Sum of calendar year decrease percentages	*Calendar year factor*
Less than 5%	12
5% or more but less than 7.5%	11
7.5% or more but less than 10%	10
10% or more but less than 12.5%	9
12.5% or more but less than 15%	8
15% or more but less than 17.5%	7
17.5% or more but less than 20%	6
20% or more but less than 25%	5
25% or more but less than 30%	4
30% or more but less than 40%	3
40% or more but less than 50%	2
50% or more but less than 60%	1
60% or more	0

4. The *experience factor* is the sum of these three factors, and this in turn determines the class to which the employer belongs. In our example, the experience factor was 15. In the following table, it can be seen that an experience factor of 15 falls in class VI (6).

Employer's experience factor	*Class*
29–28	I
27–26	II
25–23	III
22–20	IV
19–17	V
16–14	VI
13–11	VII
10–8	VIII
7–5	IX
4	X

EXHIBIT 1–5 (*concluded*)

5. The final factor in determining the contribution rate is the *state reserve ratio*—the percentage of the amount of money in the state fund (on the first day of the rate year) to the total wages of all employers for the preceding calendar year. The state computes this percentage. In our example, suppose for 1976, the state reserve ratio was 4.5 percent. Applying this to the following table (and remembering we want class VI), the 1976 contribution rate is 2.0 percent.

Contribution rate table—state reserve ratio

	Reserve percent of total wages						
	At least 6%	5 *to* 5.99%	4 *to* 4.99%	3 *to* 3.99%	2 *to* 2.99%	1.4 *to* 1.99%	*Less than* 1.4%
I......	0.7	0.9	1.0	1.1	1.4	1.7	2.7
II......	0.9	1.0	1.2	1.3	1.6	1.9	2.7
III.....	1.0	1.2	1.4	1.5	1.8	2.1	2.7
IV.....	1.2	1.4	1.6	1.7	2.0	2.3	2.7
V......	1.4	1.6	1.8	1.9	2.2	2.5	2.7
VI.....	1.6	1.8	2.0	2.1	2.3	2.7	2.7
VII....	1.8	2.0	2.2	2.3	2.4	2.7	2.7
VIII...	2.1	2.2	2.4	2.5	2.6	2.7	2.7
IX.....	2.3	2.5	2.6	2.6	2.7	2.7	2.7
X......	2.7	2.7	2.7	2.7	2.7	2.7	2.7

Tax rate notice

All states, and the District of Columbia, issue tax rate notices once a year. In its simplest terms, the rate notice indicates the following:

1. The experience used to compute the tax rate, that is, taxable payroll, contributions, benefit charges, and possibly, the account balance.
2. The ratio computed by dividing the taxable payroll *by* one of the other items.
3. Any state factors or emergency rates.
4. The tax rate for a one-year period.

Most tax rates are effective on January 1 of any year. In other words, the tax rate indicated applies to the calendar year starting with the quarter ending March 31. The only exceptions are the following:

State	*Effective quarter*
Alabama	Second quarter
Maine	Third quarter
Maryland	Third quarter
New Hampshire	Third quarter
New Jersey	Third quarter
Tennessee	Third quarter
Vermont	Third quarter

The computation date is that date through which your experience is used to compute your rate. For example, if the computation date was June 30, your 1976 tax rate would be determined on your experience through June 30, 1975.

Because your experience in taxable payroll, benefit charges, and possibly contributions, and account balance are all factors in determining your tax rate, the computation date for each of them is important and can be the same or different. See Exhibit 1–6 for a list of the computation dates for taxable payroll, benefit charges, and contributions (if applicable) for all states.

Most employers are in a quandary regarding the extent to which the rate notice should be verified. It is very simple to verify your rate notice. Many employers think rate verification is difficult, but usually they have failed to try.

All you have to do is keep a running record during the year of the individual items that are on the rate notice and see if your totals agree with the figures on the rate notice. For example, suppose you are in a reserve ratio state such as

EXHIBIT 1–6

Computation dates

	Computation date		
State	*Taxable payroll*	*Contributions*	*Benefit charges*
Alabama	12/31	—	12/31
Alaska	6/30	—	—
Arizona	6/30	6/30	6/30
Arkansas	12/31	6/30	6/30
California	12/31	6/30	6/30
Colorado	6/30	6/30	6/30
Connecticut	6/30	—	6/30
Delaware	9/30	—	9/30
District of Columbia	3/31	3/31	6/30
Florida	9/30	—	12/31
Georgia	6/30	6/30	6/30
Hawaii	12/31	12/31	12/31
Idaho	6/30	6/30	6/30
Illinois	6/30	—	6/30
Indiana	6/30	6/30	6/30
Iowa	9/30	9/30	9/30
Kansas	12/31	6/30	6/30
Kentucky	9/30	9/30	9/30
Louisiana	6/30	6/30	6/30
Maine	12/31	12/31	12/31
Maryland	12/31	—	3/31
Massachusetts	9/30	9/30	9/30
Michigan	6/30	6/30	6/30
Minnesota	6/30	—	6/30
Mississippi	6/30	—	6/30
Missouri	6/30	6/30	6/30
Montana	6/30	6/30	6/30
Nebraska	12/31	12/31	12/31
Nevada	12/31	6/30	6/30
New Hampshire	12/31	12/31	12/31
New Jersey	12/31	12/31	12/31
New Mexico	6/30	6/30	6/30
New York	9/30	9/30	12/31
North Carolina	6/30	6/30	6/30
North Dakota	12/31	12/31	12/31
Ohio	6/30	6/30	6/30
Oklahoma	12/31	—	12/31
Oregon	6/30	—	6/30

EXHIBIT 1–6 (*continued*)

State	*Computation date* — *Taxable payroll*	*Computation date* — *Contributions*	*Benefit charges*
Pennsylvania	6/30	6/30	6/30
Rhode Island	9/30	6/30	9/30
South Carolina	6/30	6/30	6/30
South Dakota	12/31	12/31	12/31
Tennessee	12/31	12/31	12/31
Texas	9/30	—	9/30
Utah	12/31	—	—
Vermont	12/31	—	12/31
Virginia	6/30	—	6/30
Washington	No experience rating		N/A
West Virginia	6/30	6/30	6/30
Wisconsin	6/30	6/30	6/30
Wyoming	6/30	—	6/30

Michigan. You know the computation date for all factors is June 30. Therefore, your tax rate is determined using your experience through June 30 of the previous year. If the state uses one year of experience and you are computing your 1976 tax rate, you would add the four quarters of taxable payroll, contributions, and benefit charges for the period 7/1/74 through 6/30/75 and see if the totals you obtained are the same figures that appear on the 1976 rate notice. If not, try and determine why. If you can't determine the reason for the discrepancy, you may then want to write a letter to the state.

Examples of rate computations for reserve ratio, benefit ratio, benefit-wage ratio, and payroll-variation types of experience rating have been given already.

Once you learn how to compute the ratio, you

will never again have a problem verifying the rate. You may ask, "Is it worth my time?" Think of it this way: if your taxable payroll is $1,000,000 and the state makes a 0.2 percent error on your rate calculation, this could cost you $2,000.

Voluntary contributions

A voluntary contribution is a payment made into your unemployment account in order to reduce your unemployment tax rate. This payment is completely voluntary and will either increase your reserve balance or cancel benefit charges. See Exhibit 1–7 for a list of states which allow voluntary contributions and the date on which they must be paid.

The employer must in all instances, except Indiana, determine the amount of money necessary for a voluntary contribution. In Indiana, the amount of money necessary to reduce the tax rate to the next lower level is indicated on the tax rate notice mailed to the employer.

CAUTION. For the states of Arizona, Nebraska, New York, and South Dakota, the voluntary contribution must be calculated and submitted *prior* to receipt of the tax rate notice. In all other states, the employer can wait until the rate notice is received prior to calculating and submitting a voluntary contribution.

You may be wondering "how do you compute a voluntary contribution?" and "will our company really save money by making a voluntary contribution and reducing our tax rate this year?" You might then add, "by paying in less money this year, won't this increase our tax rate in subsequent years?" Following is a discussion of both items.

EXHIBIT 1–7

Voluntary contributions and time limits

State	*Time limit for making voluntary contributions*
Arizona	On or before January 31.
Arkansas	Thirty days of the mailing of rate notice, but not later than March 12. *A voluntary contribution can be made only to cancel benefit charges in the year ending the previous June 30.* In other words, if you had no benefit charges for that one-year period, you cannot make a voluntary contribution.
Colorado	On or before March 14.
D.C.	Thirty days of the mailing of the rate notice, but not more than 120 days after the beginning of the year.
Indiana	Thirty days of the mailing of the rate notice, but not more than 120 days after the beginning of the year.
Iowa	On or before March 15.
Kansas	Thirty days of the mailing of the rate notice, but not more than 120 days after the beginning of the year. A reduction in tax rate by making a voluntary contribution is limited to one half of 1 percent.
Kentucky	Twenty days of the mailing of the rate notice.
Louisiana	Thirty days of the mailing of the *benefit charge* statement for the one-year period ending on the previous June 30. As in Arkansas, *a voluntary contribution can be made only to cancel benefit charges incurred during the one-year period ending June 30.* This voluntary contribution provision can be waived in any year in which increased rates due to a low fund balance are in effect. This occurred in 1975.
Maine	Thirty days of the mailing of the rate notice.
Michigan	Thirty days of the mailing of the rate notice, but not more than 120 days after the beginning of the year. Except for negative balanced employers, a voluntary contribution cannot reduce the tax rate by more than one step (increment).
Minnesota	Thirty days of the mailing of the employer's rate notice, but not more than 120 days after the beginning of the year. As in Arkansas and Louisiana, *a voluntary contribution can be made only to cancel benefit charges.*

EXHIBIT 1–7 (*continued*)

State	*Time limit for making voluntary contributions*
Missouri	On or before January 15.
Montana	Thirty days of the mailing of the rate notice. A voluntary contribution is permitted only if benefits charged to the employer's account for the last three years preceding the computation date *exceed* contributions for that same period of time.
Nebraska	On or before January 31.
New Jersey	Thirty days of the mailing of the rate notice, but *within* 120 days of the start of the rate year. The rate year in New Jersey starts July 1, rather than January 1.
New York	On or before February 1.
North Carolina	Thirty days of the mailing of the rate notice. Only 80 percent of the voluntary payment is credited to the employer's account.
North Dakota	One hundred twenty days after the beginning of the year.
Ohio	On or before December 31 of the year prior to the rate year.
Pennsylvania	Thirty days of the mailing of the rate notice, but not more than 120 days after the beginning of the year.
South Carolina	Before March 1.
South Dakota	On or before January 31.
West Virginia	Thirty days of the mailing of the rate notice.
Wisconsin	Must be paid in the period July 1 through November 30 in the year preceding the rate year.

Voluntary contribution computation

The basic item to remember when computing a voluntary contribution is "what amount of money will it take to reduce my tax rate?" If you remember that statement, you could even determine the amount of money necessary to make the voluntary contribution by trial and error. See Exhibit 1–8 for an example of the method normally used to compute the voluntary contribution.

EXHIBIT 1–8

Voluntary contribution computation

Formula

1. Average annual payroll.......... $________
2. Reserve ratio necessary for desired rate.......................... ________%
3. Account balance necessary for desired rate (multiply line 1 by line 2; drop cents and raise to next highest dollar amount)........... $________
4. Present account balance (from tax rate notice just received)......... $________
5. Amount of voluntary payment necessary to obtain the desired rate (subtract line 4 from line 3)....... $________

Example

Suppose the following conditions exist:

Contribution rate table

Reserve ratio (percent)	*Contribution rate (percent)*
Less than 2	2.7
2 but less than 3	2.4
3 but less than 4	2.2
4 but less than 5	2.0
5 but less than 6	1.6
6 but less than 7	1.3
7 but less than 8	1.0
8 but less than 9	0.8
9 and over	0.0
Average annual payroll	$120,650*
Present account balance	9,553.20*
Reserve ratio ($9,553.20 ÷ $120,650)	7.92%*
Tax rate (see preceding table)	1.0%

* Obtained from tax rate notice received.

EXHIBIT 1–8 (*continued*)

Actual computation

1.	Average annual payroll......................	$120,650.00
2.	Reserve ratio necessary for desired rate.........	8.0%
3.	Account balance necessary for desired rate (line 1 times line 2).........................	$ 9,652.00
4.	Present account balance......................	$ 9,553.20
5.	Amount of voluntary payment necessary to obtain the desired rate (line 3 minus line 4).....	$ 98.80

After determining the voluntary payment, you must decide whether it is worthwhile. In the example shown above, if the taxable payroll for the rate year in question is estimated to be $120,000, the estimated savings can be determined as follows:

$120,000	taxable payroll
0.2	reduction in tax rate from 1.0% to 0.8% in our example if voluntary payment made
$240.00	estimated gross savings
less 99.00*	amount of voluntary payment
$141.00	net savings

* $98.80 rounded to next highest dollar.

There are some points to remember:

1. Try and determine, as best as you can, if your taxable payroll is going to remain the same, will increase, or will decrease during the year for which you are calculating the voluntary payment.

   If you find that your taxable payroll is going to decrease substantially, it may not be worthwhile to make a voluntary payment.

By the same token, if you determine your taxable payroll is going to increase, it might be worthwhile to make a voluntary payment under conditions that normally would not save you money.

As an example of both situations:

a. You find a voluntary payment of $99 will reduce your tax rate by 0.2 percent and will save you a net amount of $150 based on your taxable payroll for the current year. However, you plan to cut your work force by one half next year. Under these conditions, you will not save anything by making a voluntary payment.

b. You find a voluntary payment will reduce your tax rate by 0.2 percent, but your net loss will be $150 based on your taxable payroll for the current year. However, you plan to double your work force next year. Under these conditions, you will save several hundred dollars by making a voluntary payment.

True savings

Some employers feel that even though a voluntary contribution might save a company tax dollars in the short run, the long-run savings are minimal, at best. These employers argue that because of the voluntary contribution, their tax rate is lower this year than it otherwise would have been. These employers further argue that because less money is going into their unemployment account this year because of the voluntary payment, their tax rate in subsequent years will be higher.

There is some validity to this line of thinking. Most employers, however, make the voluntary contribution for the following reasons:

1. Tax dollars come off the top. Taxes must be paid prior to any other expenditures. Therefore, a penny saved is more than a penny earned.
2. Even if the tax rate increases in subsequent years, the taxes will be paid with "cheaper" dollars than in the current year.
3. No one can exactly forecast the future. Because of future layoffs, and resultant benefit charges, the tax rate may increase anyway; therefore, the money saved by making the voluntary contribution would be a windfall. Conversely, if few benefit charges occur, the tax rate may decrease, irrespective of whether or not the voluntary contribution was made.

Because of this variance in ratios, an employer who does not make a voluntary contribution may one day regret this decision.

Changes in corporate structure

Throughout the lifetime of a corporation, many changes in the structure of the corporation can occur. A merger, sale, acquisition, new corporation, change in name, or sale of part of a business can present many headaches and problems.

Each state maintains its own regulations regarding forms to complete and transfers of experience. Millions of dollars are lost annually by corporations that do not complete necessary forms properly, or on time.

Before discussing these matters further, let's define a few terms.

Corporation—an association of individuals, created by law or under authority of law, having a continuous existence independent of the existences of its members and powers and liabilities distinct from those of its members. Each corporation stands on its own. The corporation would have in each state in which it qualifies, an unemployment experience tax rate.

Division—a part of the whole—one of the parts into which a thing is divided. In the manner in which we are speaking, a division of a corporation would be a portion or part of a corporation. *The division would have the same unemployment experience rate in a state as its parent corporation.* Thus, if XYZ Corporation had ten divisions in a state, all divisions would have the same unemployment insurance tax rate in that particular state.

Subsidiary corporation—a corporation whose controlling interest is owned by another corporation. *Note:* Many companies use the term "subsidiary" to mean a division of a corporation, we mean a separate corporation only.

Predecessor corporation—the corporation which preceded the new or succeeding entity.

Successor corporation—the corporation that succeeds to another corporation—the resultant corporation.

Suggestion. If possible, when a change in corporate structure takes place, it is most convenient at the end of a quarter. In some states, if a merger takes place at any time other than at the end of a quarter, two quarterly contribution reports must be completed—one for the period prior to the change, and one for the period subsequent to the change.

Let's now discuss each different type of change that can take place.

Name change

A name change is nothing more than what it says—a name change. You should send a letter to the state unemployment agencies involved and notify them of the name change; your tax rates will not be affected.

New corporation

Suppose a new corporation B is established. Corporation A is succeeded to in all respects by corporation B. In most states, the transfer of un-

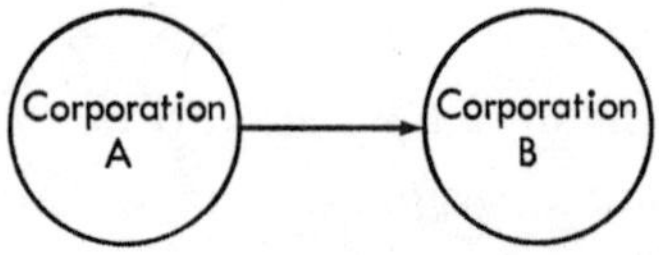

employment experience would be mandatory. This is a full and complete transfer, assuming the business keeps operating, all employees are transferred, and so on. All you need do is write a letter to the state unemployment agency indicating what took place. Or, you can wait until the end of the quarter and send the letter with your quarterly contribution report.

In those states where a full transfer of experience is not mandatory, decide immediately if you want the experience to be transferred. If so, write a letter immediately to the state involved.

A merger involves the combining of resources of at least two corporate entities. In a merger, one of the corporations will succeed to the other, or, perhaps, a new corporation will emerge as the successor.

Merger

The normal regulation regarding transfers of experience in that state would apply. If corporation A is the result of the merger of corporations B and C, the transfer of experience from B and C to A would be mandatory in most states. How-

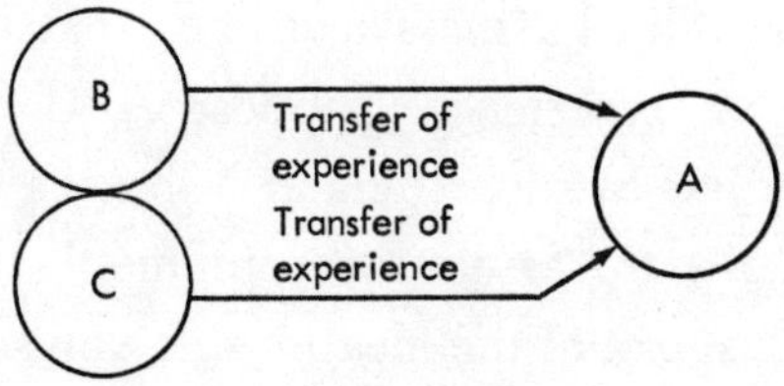

ever, check with the states. In some states, a transfer of unemployment experience is not mandatory, even if all of the assets are transferred and the business is continued without interruption.

Acquisition or sale of a business

If the stock of a company is acquired for cash or securities, the corporation has not really changed in any respect as far as the state unemployment agencies are concerned. There is no need to contact them (unless there is a name change, or other change).

However, let's look at three other possibilities:

1. Complete business acquired and merged into another company. As discussed in the merger section, check the state law. In most cases, the transfer of experience would be

mandatory. Some states require approval by the predecessor before they will transfer the experience. Therefore, this might be discussed with the predecessor prior to completion of the acquisition.

2. Complete business acquired by a corporation not previously operating in that state. As discussed in 1 above (as in mergers), the transfer of experience in most states would be mandatory. However, investigate the state regulation and act accordingly.
3. Part of the business acquired—partial transfer of experience. Suppose ABC Corporation has two locations in Nebraska and you acquire the assets and continue the business of just *one* of the locations. If you so desire, Nebraska will transfer that portion of the predecessor's experience you actually acquired. They do this based on payroll records dating back several years. They will want to know what segregated portion of the business was acquired.

   In order to achieve desired results, we recommend the following procedure:

   a. Determine if you want a portion of the predecessor's experience. Examine your predecessor's tax rates, but also determine what you are going to do with the location. Are you going to close it down? Have there been layoffs prior to the change?

   b. If you decide you want this partial transfer of experience, *write immedi-*

ately to the state agency involved. Many states impose a time limit for the successor to file an application for transfer. Also, some states require the approval of both the predecessor and successor employers before a transfer will take place.

In many states that do not allow a partial transfer of experience, after the date of acquisition, you do not need to start over in determining the taxable wage base limit of each employee. Check the regulation in that state. Starting over on the taxable wage base for each employee could needlessly cost you several thousand dollars.

For example, on 9/30/75, you acquire and continue without interruption a Missouri location of XYZ Corporation. XYZ has five other locations in Missouri. In this situation, Missouri will not allow a partial transfer of experience. However, by 9/30/75 most of the employees will have earned the taxable wage limit on which employers are taxed. There is no need for you to start over and report fourth-quarter wages as taxable wages, except for those employees who have not yet earned the taxable amount.

SUGGESTION. If you acquire or take over one location of a company that has other locations in that state, contact the unemployment agency to determine:

1. If a partial transfer of experience is allowed,
2. If you have to start over on the taxable wage base.

Corporate structures for profit

Many times, you can manipulate corporations and thereby save substantial sums of money. The following examples will illustrate.

1. You have a corporation in Texas which has been operating for several years and has the minimum tax rate of 0.1 percent. You are going to establish another corporation in Texas employing 100 people. Texas allows a partial transfer of experience. Transfer a few people from the old to the new corporation. You will then be able to transfer a portion of the experience. If the experience would not be transferred so that you will get a 0.1 percent tax rate, you would be assigned the standard tax rate of 2.7 percent for several years.

Estimated savings over three years:

100 employees × $4,200 (taxable wages/employee) = $420,000
Total taxable payroll per year = $420,000 × 3 = $1,260,000
Total taxable payroll three years = $1,260,000 × 2.7% = $34,020
Total taxable payroll three years = $1,260,000 × 0.1% = 1,260
Tax savings.............................. $32,760

You can also apply this to several corporations. Corporation A might be split into five corporations and the experience transferred.

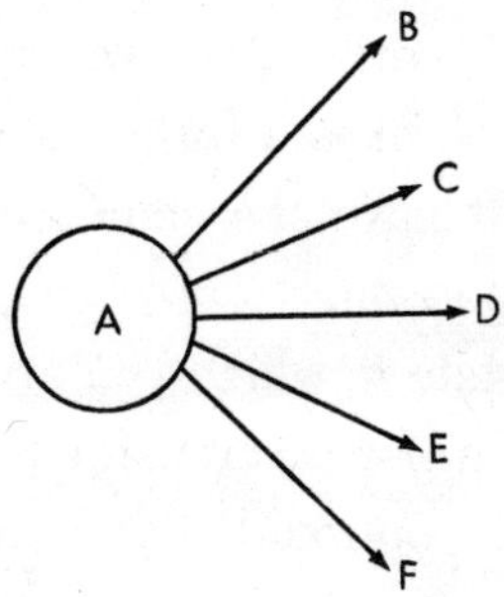

Before trying to apply this procedure, be sure and investigate the regulation in that state. Many states do not allow a partial transfer of experience.

2. You acquire or have a business that is maximum rated. Many state regulations state that if substantially all of a business is continued without interruption, a complete transfer of experience is mandatory. However, what if you were to close the business immediately upon acquisition for a few days, or a week? You may then not have continued the business without interruption, and you could start over at the standard rate, which is usually 2.7 percent.

   CAUTION. If the state suspects you are closing the business for the express purpose of reducing your tax rate, or so that you can start over at the standard rate, they may try and transfer the experience. If they try this, you can appeal any such determination.

3. Suppose the corporation in which you have your employment has a very high tax rate. Suppose further that you have either a

"dormant" corporation which has a fairly low tax rate, or you form a new corporation which will have the standard tax rate of, say, 2.7 percent.

If the state in which you are located does not allow a partial transfer (or if a partial transfer is optional), you might transfer some of your employees to the lower rated corporation. Do not transfer enough employees to force a transfer of experience. The extent to which you can transfer employees and not have to take over the experience of the high-rated company can be determined from discussing this matter with the appropriate state personnel.

Caution. In some states, if the same stockholders own more than one corporation (common ownership), the state will merge the experience of all of these corporations and the procedure described above will be ineffective.

4. You are already operating in the state of Ohio and you acquire a company that has a 3.7 percent tax rate. Your tax rate is 1.2 percent.

   a. 1.2 percent

   b. 3.7 percent

   You should determine what you are going to do with company B before you decide whether or not to merge it into A. If you plan to eventually reduce the number of employees at B (or, perhaps your predecessor laid off quite a few employees), by merging the two corporations, you would probably obtain a maximum tax rate that could possibly cost you tens of thousands of dollars annually. Better yet, you might possibly phase out corporation B, and the few employees you might want to keep could be transferred to corporation A.

5. You own a department store and have quite a few layoffs after Christmas, Easter, and so on. Because of these layoffs and resultant unemployment charges, your tax rate is not as low as it could be without these charges. Let's suppose you form corporation B and put into this corporation all temporary and part-time employees. Savings to corporation A (the company that contains all of your full-time employees) could be very substantial. If corporation A employs 300 people, a 1 percent reduction in your tax rate would save you $15,000–$20,000 annually.

Caution. This method of separating employees is commonly called "payrolling" and is frowned upon by state unemployment agencies. Also, many states contain provisions that would defeat your intended purpose. For example, as mentioned elsewhere, the regulation may contain a provision that where there is common ownership, the experience for all such corporations is combined when computing unemployment tax rates. Check the regulation in that particular state!

6. Employer A has employment only in Iowa. It is anticipated that in a year or so expansion will be made into Illinois. Further, employer A has a location site in Illinois. The standard tax rate for new employers in Illinois is 2.7 percent. The maximum tax rate is 4.0 percent, and the minimum tax rate is 0.1 percent. A new employer must pay at the 2.7 percent rate for at least three years.

   Suggestion. Employer A, because a payroll is anticipated in Illinois, should elect coverage under the Illinois unemployment regulation as quickly as possible. The wages for the employee assigned to take over the new location could be reported to Illinois.

   Result. By reporting wages to Illinois as quickly as possible, employer A will come off of the standard 2.7 percent tax rate faster than if A had waited until the location was in full employment. To come off of the standard 2.7 percent tax rate even one year sooner can result in substantial tax savings, assuming that the tax rate will decrease sooner than if this employer had waited until unemployment taxes had to be paid.

   Remember. The first year an employer comes off of the standard rate, the employer's rate may not actually decrease; however, by following the procedure just described, the tax rate will decrease faster.

7. Employer A has employment only in Iowa and anticipates that in a year or so, expansion will be made into Illinois. Employer A could start looking for a small employer in Illinois that has a very low tax rate that could be acquired. Employer A could then succeed to the other employer and enjoy a very low tax rate. As an example of the dollars employer A could save, suppose A acquires an employer with a 0.1 percent tax rate and anticipates 300 people on their payroll in Illinois.

New employer tax rate:		
300 people × 4,200 tax base =	$1,260,000	taxable payroll
New employer tax rate is.....	2.7%	
Unemployment tax paid......	$ 34,020	
Successor to 0.1 percent tax rate:		
300 people × $4,200 tax base =	$1,260,000	taxable payroll
Tax rate from predecessor.....	0.1%	
	$1,260	
Savings......................	$34,020	
Less.........................	1,260	
	$32,760	per year
	3	years standard rate applicable
Gross savings................	$98,280	

In benefit ratio and benefit-wage ratio states (see experience-rating chapter), a sudden increase in taxable payroll will *decrease* tax rates. Because Illinois is a benefit-wage ratio state, in the example cited, a sudden increase in payroll when the company is in full operation will help reduce the tax rate.

CAUTION. In reserve ratio states (see section on experience rating at the beginning of this chapter), a sudden increase in taxable payroll will tend to *increase* the tax rate a year or two later. However, electing coverage as quickly as possible can result in tax savings.

Proper reporting of taxes involving mergers

Generally speaking, when a corporation is absorbed by another corporation in a statutory merger or consolidation, the resultant entity is regarded as the same taxpayer and same employer as the absorbed corporation for payroll tax purposes. The employment, then, by the absorbed corporation to the resultant corporation, is said to continue. Accordingly, the credits against the federal unemployment tax provided by section 3302 of the 1954 Internal Revenue Code for contributions made by the absorbed corporation into state unemployment funds with respect to such employment are allowable to the resultant corporation.

Regarding employment taxes, the following guidelines can be followed:

1. Form W–2—*withholding tax statement:* One W–2 can be furnished to each employee; showing as one total the wages paid in the year of the merger by one or both corporations.
2. Form W–3—*reconciliation of income taxes withheld:* One Form W–3 should be filed by the resultant corporation; the amount of income tax withheld by each corporation need not be separately identified.
3. Form 941—*employer's quarterly federal tax return:* One Form 941 for the quarter in which the merger occurred should be filed

by the resultant corporation covering the wages paid by both corporations during this period.

4. Form 940—*employer's annual federal unemployment tax return:* One Form 940 for the year in which the merger occurred should be filed by the resultant corporation covering the wages paid by both corporations during the year.
5. *State unemployment taxes:* Depending on the requirement in each particular state, the resultant corporation does not normally have to start over on the tax base for those employees who worked for the absorbed corporation and continue to work for the resultant corporation. This is generally true whether or not the state requirement requires the merging of the unemployment experiences of the two entities and a new tax rate as of the date of acquisition or at a later date, such as the first quarter of the year following the date of merger. The first return filed by the resultant corporation subsequent to the merger or consolidation should be accompanied by information indicating that the change has taken place.

Prior to leaving this subject, a word or two should be said about whether an employer can change a corporation or organization strictly to avoid taxation. In *Weeks* v. *Sibley*, 269 Fed 155 (1920), a Federal District Court stated "that the right to change the status of an organization, or to dissolve an organization, in any legal manner, is not made ineffectual because the motive impelling the change is to reduce or avoid taxation in the future. The right to do so is an incidental right, inseparately connected with an individual's right to control his property."

This would tend to imply that there certainly is a difference between trying to avoid taxes and trying to evade taxes. Of course, as mentioned elsewhere, the state regulations involving ownership of corporations and transfers of experience may preclude the implementation of the suggestions in this section.

To summarize, by taking advantage of those parts of the unemployment regulations relating to experience rating and changes in corporate structure, substantial savings can result. We have attempted to give employers several ideas that can be pursued. Because unemployment regulations change from time to time, it is important that prior to implementation, any employer desiring to pursue these matters first obtain all the facts; especially the end result of any proposed changes in corporate structure.

Independent contractors

The relationship of workers to the person for whom they perform services influences whether they are, in fact, employees of such employer, or are independent contractors. Most of the state regulations have incorporated strict tests of what constitutes such absence of control by an employer over a worker that he or she would be classed as an independent contractor rather than an employee. Many states provide that service for remuneration is considered employment unless it meets three tests:

1. The worker is free from control or direction in the performance of his or her work under the contract of service, and in fact
2. The service is performed either outside the usual course of the business for which it is performed, or is performed outside of all places of business of the enterprise for which it is performed, and
3. The individual is customarily engaged in an independent trade, occupation, profession, or business.

The common-law master-servant relationship is the principal consideration of coverage in several states. A few states have a general definition of employment in terms of services performed—"any contract of hire, written or oral, express or implied."

It is important that all employers who have "questionable" independent contractors working for them investigate the proper Internal Revenue and/or state regulations. Such other areas as social security and workmen's compensation could be affected by an arbitrary decision to treat someone as an independent contractor.

Joint accounts and common accounts

Many states have a provision in their unemployment regulations involving what is commonly called a joint account. The term "joint account" means a joining together of two or more unemployment tax accounts. The combining of accounts would include combining taxable payrolls, benefit charges, and contributions for unemployment tax purposes only. There need not be a so-called statutory merger of corporations in order to apply for the combining of the accounts.

The following states make provision for the formation of joint accounts (also called "common account" in Ohio, and "unity of enterprise" in California):

Arizona	Hawaii	South Carolina
California	Missouri	Washington
Colorado	New Jersey	West Virginia
Connecticut	New York	Wyoming
Delaware	Ohio	

Advantages of a joint account

1. Through the combining of various accounts, overall tax payments might be less. For example:

Company A:	
Taxable payroll	$2,000,000
Account balance	400,000
Reserve ratio*	20%
Tax rate	0%
Tax payments†	$ 0
Company B:	
Taxable payroll	$ 500,000
Account balance	50,000
Reserve ratio	10%
Tax rate	0.4%
Tax payments	$ 2,000
Combining accounts of A and B:	
Taxable payroll	$2,500,000
Account balance	450,000
Reserve ratio	18%
Tax rate	0%
Tax payments	$ 0

* Reserve ratio = Account balance ÷ Taxable payroll.

† Tax payments = Tax rate × Taxable payroll.

For this example in the reserve ratio state in which both corporations are located, a reserve ratio in excess of 15 percent produces a minimum tax rate of 0 percent. The reserve ratio of company A was so far in excess of the 15 percent that the combining accounts still produced a minimum tax rate; saving $2,000 for the year.

2. Through corporate manipulation, an account with a deficit balance could possibly start over as a new employer. A joint account could be set up between several corporations and one of them could pull out in a year or two and obtain the status of a new employer, or a new corporation could be formed with employees reported to the new corporation on January 1st of any year.

   CAUTION. You must study the regulation before attempting such a joint venture in order to reduce taxes. Inquiries should be made to the state unemployment agency in order to learn all of the pertinent facts.

3. In several of the states that allow joint accounts, only one quarterly wage report need be completed, rather than one wage (contribution report) for each employer. This can save time.
4. Where applicable, when employees are transferred between corporations, the employer does not have to start over on the tax base. For example:

   Company A and company B are in a joint account. The tax base (taxable wages) in the state are a person's first $4,800 of earnings per calendar year. The tax rate for the joint account is 2 percent. Employee M works for company A until June 30 and earns $10,000. Company A would then pay the state $96 in unemployment taxes ($4,800 × 2%). Employee M then transfers to company B, a separate corporation, and the other member of the joint account. From July 1 until December 30, employee M earns $10,000.

If employers A and B *were not* members of a joint account, on July 1, when employee M transfers to employer B, employer B, being another corporation, would have to start over reporting M's wages. Employer B would have to pay $96 in unemployment taxes to the state. Because both employers are members of a joint account, they are, in effect, one employer, and employer B does not have to pay any additional taxes to the state; resulting savings equals $96.

An employer, then, who has many corporations in any of the states that allow for a joint account and constantly transfers employees from one corporation to another, could save quite a sum of money yearly through the savings described herein.

Caution. All of the states that provide for a joint account do not necessarily provide for this saving. The regulation would have to be investigated by the employer.

Disadvantages of a joint account

1. In some of the states mentioned, the decision to form a joint account is irrevocable. Once the joint account is in effect, for any of the members to withdraw is almost impossible. Also, in some states, once a joint account is in effect, it may not be able to be dissolved for several years.
2. Each member of the joint account might be liable for the unemployment contributions of the other members.
3. A severe cutback in personnel of any member of the joint account could increase the total taxes of all members.

All advantages and disadvantages of a possible joint account must be studied. The unemployment regulations must be questioned, and all possible results must be analyzed before a decision on whether to apply for a joint account is made.

chapter 2

Personnel policies and forms

Through the proper planning, design, and use of personnel policies and forms, many unemployment charges can be avoided. Forms, whether they be application forms, disciplinary notices, or a dozen other forms:

1. Provide for the orderly processing of employee actions and/or activities.
2. Facilitate personnel record keeping.
3. Eliminate unemployment compensation benefit charges.
4. Help conform with union and/or company rules.
5. Help conform with government regulations.
6. Provide management with data necessary to examination of present policies, expenses, and efficient planning for the future.

The above list of reasons could probably go on and on. Our primary concern is with reason No. 3, "to eliminate unemployment compensation benefit charges." The use and wording of a personnel form can mean the difference between being charged for a person's unemployment benefits (as much as $6,000 in some states), *or* not being charged one penny.

Most employers do not want to overburden their supervisory personnel with countless forms. The forms we will discuss are basic forms necessary to keep adequate records. The state expects the employer to keep good records; otherwise, a "your word against the claimant's word" situation develops which will not be to your benefit.

Types of separations

Basically, there are three types of separations:

1. *Voluntary quit*—action initiated by the employee who leaves your employment "of his or her own accord." Common reasons for resignations are:

    a. To accept other work.
    b. Dissatisfied.
    c. To leave area.
    d. To seek other employment.
    e. To attend school.
    f. To stay at home.
    g. To get married.
    h. Maternity.

    Normally, a person who voluntarily quits will be disqualified from receiving unemployment benefits (if you protest the claim form) until he or she removes the disqualification, that is, serves a certain number of weeks in which benefits cannot be collected, or obtains work until a certain amount of wages is earned. After the disqualification is removed, this person may then collect maximum benefits. However, the important thing to remember is: *Once a claimant is disqualified, your account may be relieved of charges, even if the claimant then collects full benefits.* In 36 states, your account should never be charged if someone is disqualified—even for one week.

When a person voluntarily quits, the "burden of proof" normally rests with the claimant to show that he or she quit with "good" cause. If the claimant cannot show that he or she quit with good cause, or with good cause attributable to the employer (depending on the regulation in that state), the claimant will be disqualified and the employer's account possibly relieved of any unemployment charge.

2. *Discharge for misconduct*—action initiated by the employer due to "a willful and wanton disregard of the employer's interests." The key word is "willful." To prove willful, the employer must prove:

    a. The employer had a rule regarding the matter that caused the claimant's dis-discharge,

    b. The employee knew about the rule, and

    c. The employee broke the rule.

The burden of proof, therefore, is on the employer to prove misconduct. In a later section, this will be completely discussed. However, the proof of these matters is as follows:

Item	*Proof*
a. Employer had a rule	Listing of rules; employee handbook.
b. Employee knew about rule	Signed acknowledgement received from employee.
c. Employee broke the rule	Disciplinary action.

Following are some reasons for discharging employees for misconduct:

a. Breaking rules.
b. Failure to follow instructions.
c. Excessive absenteeism.
d. Excessive tardiness.
e. Drinking.
f. Insubordination.
g. Dishonesty.
h. Fighting.

3. *Discharge for reasons other than misconduct*—action initiated by the employer due to:

a. Unsatisfactory work—person does not have the ability to do the work.
b. Lack of work.
c. Forced retirement.
d. Forced maternity leave of absence.
e. Forced maternity discharge.

Whether an employee voluntarily quits or is discharged for misconduct, the employer must keep complete records. It is possible for an employee to be separated and not file an unemployment claim for as long as a year to a year and a half, and your company would still be liable for the claimant's benefits.

The preventative personnel maintenance we previously emphasized will now be discussed in the form of sound personnel policies and forms. Some of the items discussed may be "brief" but they are important in controlling your unemployment compensation costs.

REMEMBER. Sound personnel policies and forms benefit the employee as well as the employer. Employees should know your rules. They should know when they have broken a rule, and should know where they stand in relation to their goals and objectives.

Preventative personnel maintenance

We have all heard much about "preventative maintenance"—a much-used and perhaps trite expression. Through preventative maintenance, the automobile is tuned so that repairs will be minimal; through preventative maintenance, machinery is tested for possible breakdowns and loss of time; through preventative maintenance in eating correctly and physical exercise, our bodies are kept healthy; and through preventative personnel maintenance, unemployment compensation charges and costs can be held to a minimum.

Proper hiring procedures, on-the-job procedures, and separation procedures will prevent unwarranted and invalid unemployment compensation charges. Substantial unemployment benefits are charged to employers, not necessarily because of unfair unemployment compensation regulations or because employers do not protest claims properly, but because employers do not employ prudent personnel policies. To establish proper personnel policies will protect you and be a hedge against excessive unemployment benefits charged to your company.

chapter 3

Hiring procedures

Preventative personnel maintenance starts with your hiring procedures. The application form, the interview, the reference investigation, and the physical examination all play a part in proper selection of employees.

Our objective here is to prevent problems before they begin. If you can reduce turnover through proper selection procedures, the resultant savings will far exceed the elimination of unemployment compensation charges.

Application

All companies use an application form. Depending on the nature of the job and requirements of the position, some application forms are very short, while others are lengthy and more complicated.

Screen your employees—verify employment history

Most employers ask a person to complete an application form but verify nothing stated by the applicant. Proper screening at the time of hire can save you future headaches. Check past employment history—check references. While a shortage of applicants may prevent you from thoroughly checking and verifying statements made by the applicant (you may just want a warm body), proper selection can prevent unnecessary unemployment compensation charges. We know of many examples of applicants falsely stating they worked for employers who never heard of them.

If you require a medical examination of all new employees (as many department stores and factories require), see that the examination is given prior to a person's employment with your company.

EXAMPLE. Department store X requires that all new employees be given a medical examination. Ms. Jean Smith goes to work for department store X on September 1, 1975. Because the company doctor is so busy, she is not given a physical examination until December 1, 1975 at which time it is found that she has heart trouble (which Ms. Smith was not aware of at the time she applied for work) and it is recommended that she be discharged. Ms. Smith is discharged, files an unemployment claim, and several hundred dollars of her benefits are charged to department store X. Why? Because there was no misconduct connected with her separation. Therefore, department store X was liable for at least a portion of her benefits. *Give prospective employees their physical examinations prior to employment.*

Many employers will not verify the statements made on an application form until the person has been employed for several years and is being considered for a big promotion. Upon investigation, the employer finds that a statement made by this person at the time of hire is found to be false, and the person is discharged. Of course, there is no misconduct, and unemployment benefits can be collected against the company. The company should have verified the statements on the application form before this person was hired.

Because of the ever-changing regulations and guidelines from various governmental and private agencies, we are not providing any examples of application forms. However, you may want to determine certain aspects of applicant's availability for work. Certain questions can be asked on the application form, or you may want to use a separate form.

Examples of questions to determine applicant's desire to limit working hours, and so on, are as follows:

1. Do you want to work:
   ( ) Full time.
   ( ) Part time.
   ( ) Holidays.
   ( ) Temporary.
   ( ) Other.
2. If you desire part-time or other type work, please indicate the days and hours you are available:
   Sunday ( ) Yes ( ) No
   Hours you *can* work____
   Monday ( ) Yes ( ) No
   Hours you *can* work____
   Tuesday ( ) Yes ( ) No
   Hours you *can* work____
   Wednesday ( ) Yes ( ) No
   Hours you *can* work____

Thursday ( ) Yes ( ) No
Hours you *can* work____
Friday ( ) Yes ( ) No
Hours you *can* work____
Saturday ( ) Yes ( ) No
Hours you *can* work____

3. If you desire only part-time work, what is the reason? ______________________
4. If scheduled by the company, do you agree to work Saturdays? ( ) Yes ( ) No
5. In the event of an emergency, do you agree to change shifts? ( ) Yes ( ) No
6. In the event of an emergency, do you agree to temporarily work in another department? ( ) Yes ( ) No

The applicant's answers to these questions will not only help you in hiring employees for particular days and times, but will give you certain commitments that may prove fruitful should certain questions arise at a later date regarding the claimant's availability for work.

The interview

Much trouble and expense can be eliminated if just a few simple suggestions are followed. At the employment interview, you should try and evaluate the applicant's aptitude, desire, and skills for performing in the position in which he or she will be placed.

1. Check references. Many employers don't. Some applicants may not be completely honest in answering your questions, and pertinent information regarding such items as absenteeism, tardiness, and work attitude can, in most instances, be obtained. Please see the following exhibits:

   a. Items to consider when establishing reference investigation procedure and/or forms. See Exhibit 3–1.

b. Telephone and/or written reference check. See Exhibit 3–2.

2. Determine the skills required for the position to be filled.
3. Give tests to determine applicant's qualifications and aptitude for the position.

EXHIBIT 3–1

Items to consider when establishing reference investigation procedure and/or forms

Following are examples of categories of questions and statements to make to the applicant's former employers:

Opening comments

The applicant named below has referred you to us. Your comments will be helpful in determining the applicant's qualifications for the available position.

(*Name of applicant*) has applied to us for a position with our company. As one of the applicant's former employers, you can help us and the applicant to determine if his (or her) background and attitudes qualify the applicant for the position.

(*Name of applicant*) has applied to us for a job as a (*name of position*). We would appreciate your help in answering some questions so that he (or she) can be better evaluated for the opening.

Your statements will be kept in strict confidence. The applicant has signed a statement authorizing our company to question former employers with regard to health, character, ability, and habits and disposition, and relieving all cooperating employers from any liability whatsoever (exact statement should be quoted, if possible).

General information

Name: (*of applicant*) ____________________

Employment date: From ____________ to ____________

(month, day, year) (month, day, year)

Starting position: ____________ *At termination* ____________

Salary: ______ per ______ *Salary:* ______ per ______

EXHIBIT 3–1 (*continued*)

Work attitudes

Please rate the applicant on the following:

	Excellent	*Above average*	*Average*	*Below average*	*Unsatis-factory*
Honesty					
Loyalty					
Attitude					
Reliability					
Courtesy					
Cooperation					
Ambition					
Ability					
Getting along with others					
Accepting supervision					
Ability to learn					
Enthusiasm					

Health and absenteeism

Was claimant's health satisfactory? Yes ______ No ______

Was claimant absent frequently? Yes ______ No ______

How many absences in last six months of employment? ______________

Was claimant always at work on time? Yes ______ No ______

Remarks: ____

____

Miscellaneous

Reason for separation ________________________________

____

Would you reemploy? Yes ______ No ______

Additional comments: ________________________________

____

________________________ Date ______________

Person completing form ______________________________

EXHIBIT 3–2

Telephone and/or written reference check

Name of applicant ____________________

Company contracted ____________________

Company address ____________________

____

Telephone no. ____________

Name of supervisor and/or
person spoken to ____________ *Title* ____________

(*Name of person*) has applied for a position with us. Applicant has given us permission to contact you to obtain his/her employment record with your company. Will you answer a few questions for us? All replies will be held in the strictest confidence.

1. On what date did applicant start working for you? ____________
2. What was applicant's position when he/she started? ____________
3. What was applicant's rate of pay when he/she started? ____________
4. What was applicant's rate of pay when he/she was separated? ____________
5. What was applicant's position when he/she separated? ____________
6. What was applicant's reason for leaving? ____________
7. While applicant was working for you, how was his/her

Please answer excellent, average, or unsatisfactory

   a. Attitude? ____________
   b. Cooperation? ____________
   c. Attendance? ____________
   d. Tardiness? ____________
   e. Ambition? ____________
   f. Response to criticism? ____________
   g. Ability to learn? ____________
   h. Enthusiasm? ____________
   i. Quality of work? ____________
   j. Initiative? ____________
8. Was applicant's health good? Yes ____ No ____

EXHIBIT 3–2 (*continued*)

9. Did applicant complain much? Yes ______ No ______
10. Did applicant make suggestions? Yes ______ No ______
11. Did applicant get along well with others? Yes ______ No ______
12. Would you reemploy applicant? Yes______ No ______

Additional comments: ______________________________
____

Signed ______________________ Date ________________

Unemployment benefits collected by a person separated because the person does not have the aptitude and/or the ability to do the work assigned will be charged to you. There is no misconduct. Therefore, it is important that you match a person's skills with the person's work assignment; otherwise, you will eventually terminate this person with the subsequent unemployment benefits chargeable to you.

See Exhibit 3–3 for an example of an applicant interview sheet that can be completed during or after the interview.

Temporary and part-time employees

One of our objectives in helping you control your unemployment compensation taxes is to try and eliminate from your payroll those people who will, in all likelihood, file for unemployment benefits chargeable to your company.

The temporary and/or part-time employee is the type of person who will probably file for

EXHIBIT 3–3

Applicant interview sheet

Date: ________________

Name: ____

Job classification: ____________ *Skills needed:* ________________

____

Quality Rating

	Excellent	*Good*	*Average*	*Unsat.*
First impression				
Education				
Prior work				
Knowledge of position				
Potential				
Interest in advancement				
Dedication				
Verbal expression				
Maturity				
Personality				
Overall impression				

If applicable:

1. Will applicant travel? Yes _______ No _______
2. Will applicant relocate to another location? Yes _______ No _______
3. Will applicant relocate to another city? Yes _______ No _______
4. Are applicant's hours of work restricted? Yes _______ No _______

Do you recommend applicant to be hired? Yes _______ No _______

If "No," reason: ____

____

If "Yes," reason: ____

____

Starting date: ________________ *Position:* ________________

Rate of pay: ______________ *To report to:* ________________

EXHIBIT 3–3 (*continued*)

What promise was made regarding:

1. Advancement ______________________________
2. Salary increases __________________________
3. Bonuses __________________________________
4. Profit sharing ____________________________

Comments: __________________________________

____

____

Interviewer ____________________ Dept. ________________

unemployment benefits. Part-time employees may even collect benefits at the same time they are working for you. This may sound hard to believe, but here is how this could happen: Employee J. Jones works for you 12 hours per week and earns $36 per week. Jones files for unemployment approximately four or five months after going to work for you. Jones's weekly benefit amount is usually based on the wages earned during the year to year and a half prior to the filing of the unemployment claim. Suppose Jones's benefit amount was determined to be $50 per week. Each week Jones files for unemployment, the state unemployment agency will subtract the earnings from the weekly benefit amount. In this example:

$50	weekly benefit amount
36	earnings each week subtracted
$14	unemployment benefits received and chargeable each week

Each state has its own formula for subtracting wages from unemployment benefits. Some states add $10, or another amount, to the weekly benefit amount and then subtract earnings. In this example:

$50	weekly benefit amount
10	added
$60	
36	earnings each week subtracted
$24	unemployment benefits received and chargeable each week

Still other states subtract earnings in excess of a certain percentage of the weekly benefit amount, for example, 40 percent. In this example:

$50	weekly benefit amount		
40%			
$20		$36	earnings
		20	subtracted
		$16	subtracted from weekly benefit amount
$50	weekly benefit amount		
16	subtracted		
$34	unemployment benefits received and chargeable each week		

The $14 per week, $24 per week, or $34 per week, may not sound like much money. However, suppose that person collects benefits for 20 weeks. These figures then become $280, $480, and $680 respectively. *And,* if more than one person is collecting these so-called "partial benefits," these figures can be multiplied proportionately.

The same problem exists for employees hired on a temporary basis. Suppose you needed ten extra employees for ten weeks, and each was earning only $100 per week. At the end of ten weeks, they are laid off and file for unemployment benefits. Suppose further that in the state in which they are employed, the employer can be charged one third of the person's wages for unemployment benefits. Let's see what this can cost:

10 employees @ $100 per week	$ 1,000	per week
Employed for	10	weeks
Gross wages	$10,000	
Unemployment liability, ⅓	0.333	
	$ 3,333	

Therefore, you may have budgeted $10,000 in wages for this temporary job, but the actual cost was $13,333. Of course, you also added to this cost social security, unemployment taxes (the tax actually paid to the state), and other fringe benefits.

The greatest effect on your employment taxes may not be the $3,333 that will be charged to your unemployment account, but the *effect* this will have on your tax rate for the following year. Suppose you had a taxable payroll of $500,000 (100 people times $5,000 per person), and the $3,333 in charges increased your tax rate by 1 percent. For the following year, then, your taxes would increase by $5,000 (1% × $500,000). You may now be saying, "I know part-time and temporary help is expensive, but get to the point. What can I do to hold these costs down?"

Controlling unemployment compensation charges for part-time employees starts with proper allocation of work and hiring procedures.

SUGGESTIONS

1. Instead of hiring extra employees, schedule overtime work for your present employees. The overall cost may be less, and your regular employees will earn extra money.
2. Consider the use of a temporary help service. Remember, the temporary help service doesn't pay many fringe benefits and the use of such a service may actually save you money in the long run.
3. Hire high school and college students, if possible. Some may file for unemployment benefits, but most are not eligible to collect these benefits, or are not interested.
4. Especially for a temporary position, do not tell the person the job will last for only ten weeks, or whatever. First of all, you may have some especially good temporary employees you would like to stay on. Second, some of these people may quit, possibly relieving your account of any unemployment charges, rather than being laid off for lack of work. An example of this would be summer work for college students. An incorrect hiring (and termination) procedure would be to tell prospects you will hire them for the summer and then lay them off because of lack of work on September 1st. Those who drop out of school, are unemployed the following summer, or go to school part time, may qualify for unemployment benefits—all chargeable to you.

   The correct procedure would be to tell an

applicant you have an opening and at the end of summer he or she can quit to return to school. Then, should the student file for unemployment, he or she would have quit, resulting in a disqualification rather than being laid off because of lack of work without any subsequent disqualification.

5. If a 24-per-hour per week position is available, hire one person who will work 24 hours per week rather than two people who will each work 12 hours per week. The two people who each work 12 hours per week will probably be eligible to collect unemployment benefits; the person who works 24 hours per week would probably have earned too much in wages to collect benefits.
6. Hire moonlighters and others who will most likely not file for unemployment benefits.

Think through the various alternatives and the pros and cons of each. The best solution may be a combination of the ideas we have presented, or other ideas you may have. Because of the large potential for unemployment benefit charges, the responsible manager will investigate every alternative before deciding the best course to follow.

chapter 4

Conditions of hiring

We have already discussed how important it is for employers to keep accurate and complete records. The employer who keeps good records will, in most instances, be able to prove misconduct—the employer who does not keep good records will not be able to prove misconduct. It is as simple as that!

To set down in writing conditions of hire not only protects the employer but informs the employee of what is expected of him or her and lets all concerned know rules, policies, grounds for discharge, and so on.

Misconduct

The term "misconduct" means different things to different people. Normally, as discussed previously, it means "a *willful* disregard of the employer's interests." The key word is "willful"—something someone does "on purpose"—the employee knew better but did it anyway.

The fact that you discharge someone for misconduct means nothing at an unemployment hearing unless you can *prove,* in fact, that misconduct was committed. In order to prove misconduct, that is, a willful disregard of your interests, you must prove:

1. You had a rule regarding that particular matter,
2. The employee knew about the rule, and
3. The employee broke the rule.

There is no "either-or" principle here—all three of the items must be proven by the employer. The burden of proof is on the employer's shoulders.

If you discharge someone for "alleged" misconduct which cannot be proven, an unemployment claim will almost certainly result in an excessive and possibly unnecessary unemployment charge to your company, all because you did not have employee rules, could not prove the employee knew of your rules, or that the employee broke such rules. Again, we stress proper documentation. Most employers, whose employees work under union contracts, have no problem proving misconduct when a union employee is involved because of the difficulty in discharging a union employee. All acts leading to the final act of misconduct must be well documented or the employer will not be able to discharge the employee. But, what about the supervisor who is not in a union—what about the probationary employee who has not yet joined the union, and what about nonunion office and clerical help? Many employers forget that these people can also file for unemployment and that "alleged" misconduct is not sufficient. Misconduct for these people also must be proven.

Employee rules and handbook

Work rules can be defined as a:

1. Definition of employees' rights.
2. Guideline for management disciplinary action.
3. Protection against unemployment charges.

Both the employee and the employer benefit from work rules. The employee knows where he or she stands, and the employer has defined the work rules.

The existence of work rules allows a harmonious relationship between employer and employee. Work rules allow both parties to achieve common goals. Work rules result in order instead of chaos, clarity instead of misunderstanding, respect instead of contempt, and diligence instead of indifference. For the following reasons, work rules should be in writing, not verbal!

1. Rules given verbally can be stated in different ways by different people. The manner in which a written rule is presented never varies.
2. A person can never deny that he or she was aware of a written rule. If you discuss a rule and do not put anything in writing, the knowledge of the rule can always be denied. This might affect the outcome of an unemployment, workman's compensation, or NLRB hearing.
3. A written rule is usually reviewed once every year or two—a verbal rule, almost never. Thus, as years go by, written rules become more refined and current, while verbal rules remain stagnant.

4. An employee who has broken a *known* rule has, in most cases, committed misconduct. To be able to prove misconduct at an unemployment hearing, you might have to prove a rule was broken, and you must be able to prove there was a rule in the first place. The best manner in which to prove there was a rule is to produce a written evidence of such a rule or rules. As stated above, a verbal rule or instruction can be misunderstood and denied at a later date. Knowledge of a written rule cannot be denied. And, evidence of a written rule can very well help win your unemployment protest.

Work rules are generally divided into three categories:

1. Rules of conduct.
2. Sanitation rules.
3. Safety rules.

Following is a discussion of each of these categories:

Rules of conduct

In order for companies to grow and prosper (which benefits both employer and employee), rules of behavior must be established in writing. These are usually common-sense instructions which allow employees to work together in a harmonious manner. Failure of an employee to observe these rules can result in chaos, misunderstandings, and disorder. A good set of written rules of conduct can save you grief and aggravation.

Sanitation rules

If a company produces a product consumed by the public, or by animals, or one used in medicine or the like, the product must be completely safe. The government is also interested in the safety and cleanliness of your product. Depending on what you produce, you should check government regulations.

Safety rules

Every employer wants the plant and office to be safe for the workers. Millions of dollars are spent annually to provide safe working conditions for workers. The government, through the Occupational Safety and Health Act (OSHA), has enacted safety rules and regulations for employers. In many instances, the causes of industrial accidents are the result of unsafe acts, lack of attention to the job and safety rules, and carelessness in observing the working conditions at that moment.

Exhibit 4–1, "Company Rules and Policies," indicates over 50 rules you may want to consider for your employees. A separate chapter could be written about each of these rules; however, they are self-explanatory. When developing your own company rules, you may want to distribute to your employees a more lengthy explanation of each rule. Our primary concern in proving "mis-

EXHIBIT 4–1
Company rules and policies

The following rules were developed for the mutual benefit of the employees and XYZ Corporation. The rules are intended to define acceptable rules of conduct so that cooperation will be maintained. Our purpose is not to restrict your rights, but to protect them.

Violation of the following rules will result in corrective action—from reprimand to immediate discharge (depending on the seriousness of the infraction and the frequency of occurrence).

EXHIBIT 4–1 (*continued*)

You will be violating our rules and will be disciplined (possibly resulting in discharge) if you:

1. Falsify your employment application.
2. Punch another person's timecard.
3. Fail to punch or alter your own timecard.
4. Smoke in unauthorized areas.
5. Are excessively tardy. "Excessive" means, 2 times within 5 consecutive working days, or 4 times within 30 consecutive working days.
6. In the event of illness, fail to contact the personnel department prior to scheduled working time.
7. In the event of illness, fail to contact the personnel department *each* day of your illness.
8. Are excessively absent. "Excessive" means 5 days within any 90 consecutive working days.
9. Are absent three consecutive working days without calling in.
10. Are absent four working days within a one-year period without calling in.
11. Fight, or engage in horseplay, on company premises.
12. Drink any alcoholic beverage during working hours.
13. Report to work under the influence of alcohol.
14. Are insubordinate.
15. Have unauthorized firearms and/or weapons in your possession.
16. Leave your work area without permission.
17. Leave plant during working hours without permission.
18. Receive personal telephone calls.
19. Place personal telephone calls.
20. Gamble on company property.
21. Sleep on the job.
22. Fail to observe designated parking areas.
23. Deliberately destroy company property, including tools, equipment, machinery, and vehicles.
24. Loaf.
25. Fail to punch timecard in and out properly.
26. Are guilty of theft or removal from the premises without proper authorization any company or employee property.

EXHIBIT 4–1 (*concluded*)

27. Make mistakes due to carelessness.
28. Enter restricted areas without permission.
29. Solicit contributions for any purpose unless approved by personnel department.
30. Are guilty of immoral conduct.
31. Post or remove any item from bulletin board without permission of personnel department.
32. Distribute printed items on company property without permission from personnel department.
33. Threaten or intimidate any employee.
34. Are guilty of poor housekeeping.
35. Contribute to unsanitary conditions.
36. Restrict or attempt to cause or convince others to restrict production.
37. Fail to report on "date of return" from leave of absence.
38. Fail to return when recalled from layoff.
39. Give confidential company information to unauthorized personnel.
40. Perform unauthorized work on company time.
41. Loiter before or after work on company premises.
42. Fail to report to personnel department an injury (to yourself or a fellow employee) on the day of such injury.
43. Fail, as a female employee, to notify the personnel department that you are pregnant and obtain doctor's statement.
44. Use company property for personal use.
45. Improperly use or take advantage of discount privileges.
46. Fail to observe designated dress regulations.
47. Fail to give proper receipt to customers.
48. Are careless in using cash register.
49. Are discourteous to customers.
50. Fail to obey safety rules.
51. Distract others through shouting, screaming, or demonstrations on company premises.
52. Make false or malicious statements concerning any employee or the company.
53. Use abusive language to any employee or customer.
54. Fail to follow instructions.

conduct" is to prove first of all that you had a listing of rules of conduct.

Work rules—miscellaneous suggestions

1. *Rules must be reasonable.* We knew an employer who had a rule that "anyone who is one minute tardy is subject to discharge." This is, of course, unreasonable. Normally, to be reasonable, a rule (and subsequent disciplinary action) must show a direct connection between the act of the employee and a risk to the employer's business.
2. *You must prove your employees were aware of your rules.* The second requirement for proving misconduct is "the employee must know about your rules." This is easily said, but often fails in practice. Many employers either do not put rules in writing (rules sometimes stated verbally to employees), or distribute rules in procedural manuals for supervisory personnel. This latter procedure does no good if the employees are not given these same rules.

   The only foolproof method to prove an employee knew about your rules is to put them in writing and give them to all new employees. Further, the employee should sign a statement acknowledging that he or she received them and agrees to abide by them. See Exhibit 4–2 for an example of such a document. The rules can also be part of your employee handbook and/or can be posted. However, the best procedure is still to physically hand the new employee the

EXHIBIT 4–2

Employee acknowledgement of work rules

On ______(date)______, I was given, and read my own personal copy of the *XYZ Company Rules and Policies.* Further, I agree to abide by these rules and understand that failure to abide by them is grounds for disciplinary action.

Signed ____________________

Date ____________________

listing of rules and ask him or her to sign an acknowledgement form.

3. *Company rules and policies should be written for salaried and nonunion personnel, as well as for union personnel.* Anyone employed by you can file for unmployment benefits. Failure to provide rules for all employees will result in failure to prove misconduct when the need arises.
4. *Employee handbook.* Most large companies provide an employee handbook for all new employees. Many companies have threatened to write a handbook but have just not gotten around to doing it. There are many reasons for having an employee handbook: for some companies, it is to establish good public relations; for others, they want employee rules to be discussed, as well as the general company objectives.

Our purpose in suggesting an employee

handbook is that the employee rules we talked about previously can be incorporated into such a handbook, and the rules are not as conspicuous and may not get anyone's "dander up" as they might if there was just a list of rules passed out to each new employee. Many companies, upon request, will send you a copy of their employee handbook. On your letterhead, you can write the following letter to companies of your choice.

GENTLEMEN:

We are contemplating the issuance of an employee handbook for all of our employees.

Because of our desire to obtain examples of employee handbooks from employers in our industry (or, employers in our range of numbers of employees), we are requesting your help. We would appreciate a copy of your employee handbook for our review.

Thank you.

chapter 5

Regular personnel policies

Even though the reduction and control of unemployment taxes is our goal, the benefits you will derive from the personnel policies we will now discuss will transcend this goal. Once an individual is hired, good, sound personnel policies for everyday situations will help facilitate a productive and efficient workforce.

Probationary evaluation

In most states, if a new employee is separated for unsatisfactory work, the separating employer will be liable for at least a portion of the employee's unemployment benefits. *Unsatisfactory performance is not considered misconduct*—there is no willful disregard of the employer's interests; the employee just couldn't do the work.

Many employers are under the misconception that if an employee is separated within a certain period of time, the employer has no unemployment compensation liability and can, therefore, separate the employee for any reason and not be charged for unemployment benefits. This is not true! You may have a union probationary period of 30 or 60 days; however, this has nothing to do with the state unemployment regulations. Except

EXHIBIT 5–1

States in which the employer will not be charged for unemployment benefits *if* the following conditions exist:

State	Condition
Florida	Employer paid claimant less than $40
Minnesota	Employer paid claimant less than $520
Missouri	Employer paid claimant less than $120
	or
	Claimant employed 21 consecutive calendar days or less. In order to eliminate a charge, the first and last dates of a person's employment must be indicated on the quarterly wage report submitted to the state.
New Hampshire	Claimant employed not more than four consecutive weeks
Vermont	Claimant paid less than $595
Virginia	Claimant employed less than 30 days
West Virginia	Claimant employed less than 30 days

for the few states mentioned in Exhibit 5–1, you are liable for some portion of a person's unemployment benefits if the person works for you only one day! Therefore, unless a new employee is discharged for misconduct, there will not be a disqualification should the employee file for unemployment benefits; and you will be charged for the employee's unemployment benefits just as though the employee had been laid off because of lack of work.

Probationary period

A regular probationary period should be employed so that the new employee can be evaluated in a set period of time. The probationary period should be long enough to give you and the new employee a fair evaluation, but should be short enough so that unemployment charges are held to a minimum. The amount of money you will be charged for unemployment benefits will depend on the total wages you pay to someone. *Therefore, the longer you employ someone, the more wages you will pay, and the more you will have to pay for unemployment benefits.* A formal probationary period forces supervisors to decide whether someone should continue to be an employee, or should be discharged. The supervisor is forced to make a decision. As an example of what discharging employees because of unsatisfactory work can cost you, consider the following: Suppose over the year, 20 new employees who earn $150 per week are discharged for unsatisfactory work. Each of the 20 worked four weeks. Suppose, further, the liable employers in the state are charged 33⅓ percent of the gross wages paid to someone.

20 employees @ $150 per week =	$ 3,000	per week in wages
Times	4 weeks	
	$12,000	total wages
Times the liability of . .	33⅓%	
Unemployment charges	$ 4,000	

For just 20 employees, separated after four weeks of employment, this employer was charged $4,000 in unemployment benefits. Further, suppose 15 of the 20 employees could have been separated just one week sooner. This employer would have saved $750 because total wages would have been reduced by $2,250 (15 × $150). One third of this amount is $750. How many of us keep employees on the payroll too long? How many of us procrastinate on making a decision? To procrastinate, then, not only costs additional wages and results in less than optimum efficiency but can cost substantial sums in unemployment benefits. Sometimes procrastination takes the following forms:

1. "We knew on the 20th day that we didn't want to keep this employee, but since he (or she) didn't have to join the union until the 30th day, we discharged this employee on the 29th day."
2. "We knew on Monday that this employee wasn't satisfactory, but since payday wasn't until Friday, we waited until Friday to fire him (or her)."

Both examples are very common—and are very costly.

RECOMMENDATIONS

1. Establish a probationary period, preferably as short as possible.
2. Develop a *probationary evaluation form* to be completed by the supervisor.
3. Once a decision is made to terminate someone, it will be better for all concerned if the separation takes place as quickly as possible.

See Exhibit 5–2 for an example of a probationary evaluation form. For some employers, this type of form is given by the personnel department to the supervisor a few days prior to the evaluation date. Other employers ask the supervisors to keep a supply at their desks and keep their own records as to when probationary evaluations should take place.

EXHIBIT 5–2

Probationary period evaluation

Name ____________________ *Location worked* ____________________

Department ____________________ *Position* ____________________

Date employed ____________________ *Probationary period* (check one):

20 days ____ 60 days ____

30 days ____ 90 days ____

TO BE RETURNED TO (PERSON OR DEPARTMENT) PRIOR TO PROBATIONARY PERIOD CHECKED

Item	*Evaluation*					*Comments*
	Superior	*Above Average*	*Average*	*Fair*	*Poor*	
Quality of work						
Quantity of work						
Attitude						
Dependability						
Cooperation						
Reaction to suggestions						
Knowledge of job						
Accuracy						
Use of working time						
Absenteeism						
Tardiness						
Appearance						
Disposition						
Housekeeping						
Ability to learn						
Courtesy						
Safety habits						
Leadership ability						

What qualities impress you most about this person? ____________________

EXHIBIT 5–2 (*continued*)

What are this person's major weak points? ____________________

____

____

Should employee:

____ be retained, or

____ be dismissed

Explain ____________________________________

____

Other comments: ______________________________

____

____

Person completing form ________________ Date __________

Personnel Department

Approved ________________ Date ________________

Disapproved ________________ Date ________________

Reason ____________________________________

____

Signed ________________ Date ________________

CAUTION. In too many instances, employers treat the separation of any new employee as "unsatisfactory work" separations. This is normally done because:

1. The person has not yet joined the union and misconduct does not have to be proven in order to discharge someone. The employer can discharge a person for no particular reason.
2. The unemployment compensation cost has not been considered.

What we are saying is this: if possible (and, of course, if you have the grounds), establish misconduct on a new employee the same as you would on older employees. If a new employee is chronically tardy, warn him or her in writing—the same as you would an older employee. Through proving misconduct, you may then alleviate some, or all, of any unemployment compensation charges after the employee is separated.

Leaves of absence

Most employers, at one time or another, will give some of their employees a leave of absence for one reason or another, that is, illness, maternity, extension of vacation, or other personal reasons.

When revising or considering your leave of absence policy, there is one cardinal rule to follow: *A leave of absence should be requested by the employee in his or her writing.* Suppose you gave someone a *verbal* leave of absence and the person didn't return on the date you were told he or she would return. You wait a few days and because the person does not contact you, you replace this person. Finally, two weeks later, he or she returns and demands the job back. You tell the person that because he or she didn't return on the expected date you hired a replacement. The person promptly files for unemployment benefits and tells the unemployment agency you said (when the leave was approved) that he or she could return at any time. The state would ask you to produce a record proving the date he or she was to return. Of course, you cannot do this and must, therefore, pay the unemployment claim. Had you asked the person to request the leave of absence in writing; indicating beginning date and date of return (we don't recommend using the term "ending date"—too ambiguous), and signed by the employee, in all likelihood the state would rule the person voluntarily quit because of failure to return on the date he or she said. Failure to follow our recommended procedure could cost you hundreds, or even thousands of dollars. Exhibit 5–3 is an example of a leave of absence form to be completed by the employee.

EXHIBIT 5–3

Request for leave of absence

Name ______________________________ *Department* ____________

(last) (first) (middle)

Payroll number ____________ *Position* ________________

I am applying for a leave of absence for the following reason: ____

____

First day off ________________ *Date of return* ____________

It is my understanding that failure to return on the "date of return," or failure to obtain a written approval for an extension of the leave, will be considered a voluntary termination without notice.

Employee's signature ______________________ Date ____________

Approval recommended ____________________ Date ____________

(Supervisor)

or

Approval denied __________________________ Date ____________

(Supervisor)

(If personnel department must approve or deny, another section could be added.)

Copy No. 1—to employee

Copy No. 2—to personnel department

CAUTION. A leave of absence is also a promise that upon the return of the employee, he or she can once again work for you. Upon the employee's return, if no work is available, the employee is, in effect, being laid off and will collect unemployment compensation.

CAUTION. Many employers have a leave of absence form completed by supervisor rather than by the employee requesting the leave. If the form is completed in duplicate (or triplicate), with copies going to the employee (at which time the employee signs your copy), the union, and the company, you might have sufficient evidence that the employee agreed to the conditions stated on the form. However, we still feel it is best to have the initial request for a leave of absence requested by the employee in a written request.

Absenteeism and tardiness

Absenteeism

In many instances, employers do not have effective or established rules and policies regarding absenteeism, especially for office or salaried personnel. As you know, chronic absenteeism can cause you large sums of money in lost time and production delays. When someone has been chronically absent *and the absences have been reported properly* (in accordance with company rules) and you discharge this person, you will normally be liable for his or her unemployment benefits. Most state unemployment agencies are of the opinion that if someone reports his or her absences in accordance with company rules, there is *no* misconduct. The only possibility of winning an unemployment case when someone has properly reported his or her absences would be to have a written policy that so many absences within a stated period of time would not be tolerated. Then, when the employee is one absence away from being discharged, warn the employee in writing. But what about the person who does not report absences properly? You will probably win the unemployment case if you:

1. Explain in writing to all new employees the proper procedure to follow when they are going to be absent. It is very important that you explain *which* department the employees are to call, *who* they are to talk to when absent, and the time by which they are to call. This procedure sounds, and is, simple—but, you would be surprised how many unemployment compensation protests are lost because the employer does not have a written procedure for reporting tardiness and absences.

   EXAMPLE. Joe files an unemployment claim. He states he was discharged because he didn't report an absence. He swears he called his employer the day he was absent. At the hearing, the referee asks his employer, "How are employees to report absences?" The employer states, "The employee is to call his foreman if he is going to be absent." Joe says, "I was told by my foreman that I could call and tell the telephone operator when I was going to be absent." The referee will now ask the employer, or the claimant, "Is there anything in writing that tells the employee whom to telephone if he is going to be absent?" If the answer is, "There is nothing in writing," the employer will probably lose the protest and be charged—possibly several thousand dollars.

In the above example, had there been a simple form such as we recommend, there would have been no question as to who this man should have called when he could not come to work. See Exhibit 5–4 for an example of a form to be given to new employees, explaining their responsibilities when absent.

2. Explain to new employees disciplinary action to be taken if absences are not reported properly and/or excessive absenteeism persists. See Exhibit 5–4.
3. Explain, in writing, to all new employees that unreported absences will not be tolerated. Explain, in writing, that if an employee has two (2) or three (3) *consecutive* working days of unreported absences, you will assume the employee has abandoned his or her job and voluntarily quit.
4. Keep records of unreported absences. Most employers keep good records of a person's absenteeism when he or she calls in; however, they forget to keep a record of *unreported absences.* Employers can successfully maintain records by one of two methods:

   a. The telephone operator, personnel de-

EXHIBIT 5–4
Reporting absences

If you are going to be absent from work, you must notify your department supervisor at least 30 minutes prior to your starting time. If your supervisor is not available, contact the guard station. (Alternatives:

—Contact the personnel department

—Contact Mr. (or Ms.)____________________)

When calling to report an intended absence, you must give the following information:

1. Name of employee.
2. Clock number.
3. Department where you work.
4. Reason for absence.
5. Expected date of return.

You must call in each day of your absence.

Failure to observe these rules will result in the following disciplinary action:

First offense.............Written warning
Second offense..........One (1) day off
Third offense...........Three (3) days off
Fourth offense..........Discharge

Three consecutive working days of unreported absence will be considered a voluntary quit, that is, abandonment of your job.

partment, or guard station can keep a book and "log in" all telephone calls received (see Exhibit 5–5). The absence of someone's name on a particular day would indicate this person did not report his or her intended absence properly.

b. A form can be completed by the tele-

EXHIBIT 5–5

Log of absences

Name of employee	*Date of call*	*Time of call*	*Person calling*	*Reason for absence*	*Date of return*	*Person receiving call*

phone operator, supervisor, or personnel department, indicating the employee did not call in (see Exhibit 5–6). The form can then be filed in the employee's personnel folder for future use, if necessary.

You must keep good records or you will pay excessive unemployment taxes.

5. Do not waiver from the above rule. As you have heard, when an employer allows an exception to a rule, the exception becomes the rule.
6. Discharge the employee immediately upon breaking the rule that calls for his or her discharge. If an employee breaks the established rule, discharge him or her immediately. The state will always ask you what

EXHIBIT 5–6

Absentee report (*to be completed for every absence—reported and unreported*)

Reported ____________ Unreported ____________

Date ________

Name of person absent ____________ Dept. ________

Person calling ____________ Clock number ________

Shift ________

Reason for absence: ____________

____

____

Expected date of return ____________

To be paid ____________ Not to be paid ________

Signed ____________ Position ________

happened on the last day. If the employee has broken the rule and you let the employee return for a day or two before discharging him or her, the state will rule that there was no misconduct and you will then be liable for the employee's unemployment benefits.

Tardiness

No employer wants to tolerate constant tardiness. An employee who is constantly late to work causes increased record keeping, loss of production, and can even cause dissatisfaction among the other employees.

In order to alleviate this problem, follow these steps:

1. Establish a written policy. For example, "Three days of tardiness within a one-month period can result in your separation. If you are going to be late to work, telephone your supervisor (or whomever) at least 30 minutes prior to starting time."
2. Keep records. Every time someone is tardy, note your file.
3. Reprimand employee in writing.
4. Discharge promptly. If the employee has been tardy beyond your tolerance level, discharge the employee—and do it on the day he or she is tardy. If you have warned the employee in writing, stating that if one more tardy occurs, he or she is subject to discharge, and the employee is tardy again, discharge should occur on that day. Do not wait until you find a replacement. This will weaken your case against the employee should he or she file an unemployment claim.

Doctor's statement or medical release

In order to halt chronic absenteeism, one of the most effective methods can be to ask the employee for a doctor's statement.

A written policy should be established. For example, you could request that anyone absent for three (3) or more consecutive working days return with a doctor's statement before being permitted to return. Or, a more effective policy might be to state, upon hire, that the company can request a doctor's statement for *any* illness, whatever the length of the absence.

Disciplinary action

Remember, in order to prove misconduct, you must prove:

1. You had a rule,
2. The employee knew about the rule, and
3. The employee broke the rule.

Items 1 and 2 have already been discussed. To prove the employee broke a rule, you must prove that disciplinary action was initiated when the rule was broken.

Many employers have what is called a "progressive" disciplinary action procedure—"progressive" meaning that each subsequent violation of the same rule carries a stiffer penalty. For example, your disciplinary procedure for someone who constantly parks his or her car in the wrong space might be:

First offense.............. Verbal warning
Second offense............ Written warning
Third offense............. Three days off
Fourth offense............ Discharge

Each violation of the rule, then, carries a more severe penalty.

In Chapter 4, Exhibit 4–1 listed examples of

various rules an average employer might consider. If the employer was interested in a progressive disciplinary procedure, the penalties that would result from breaking the rules should be made known to the employees.

See Exhibit 5–7 for an example of a format that could be used to indicate to employees particular rules and disciplinary action to be taken if the rules are broken. The rules indicated are the same rules used in Exhibit 4–1, Chapter 4. Most union agreements make provision for a systematic sequence of disciplinary action to be taken when an employee breaks a rule, commits an act of misconduct, or causes trouble on the job. Usually, this action eventually involves a written letter of warning to the employee.

The above-described procedure is the best protection you have. *Always warn employees in writing*—whether they be union or nonunion employees. See Exhibits 5–8 and 5–9 for two examples of disciplinary action forms. As an alternative, a simple warning letter will suffice. What usually results when warnings are not in writing is as follows: John Simmons, a lathe operator for company A was verbally warned by his supervisor on January 8, 1975. On January 20, 1975, John committed the same act and was discharged. He did not file an unemployment claim, but immediately found another job with company B; where he remained for six months. On June 23, 1975, he was laid off because of a lack of work and filed an unemployment claim. Company A received a claim form and protested, stating he had been warned on January 8, 1975 and was discharged for misconduct on

EXHIBIT 5–7

Rules and disciplinary action

Rules	*Penalties*			
	First offense	*Second offense*	*Third offense*	*Fourth offense*
1. Falsification of employment application	Discharge			
2. Punching another person's timecard.	Discharge			
3. Failure to punch, or altering, your own timecard.	Discharge			
4. Smoking in unauthorized areas.	Warning	Discharge		
5. Excessive tardiness—2 times within 5 consecutive working days, or 4 times within 30 consecutive working days.	Warning	3 days off	Discharge	
6. In the event of illness, failing to contact the personnel department prior to scheduled working time.	Warning	Discharge		

EXHIBIT 5–7 (*continued*)

	Penalties			
Rules	*First offense*	*Second offense*	*Third offense*	*Fourth offense*
7. In the event of illness, failing to contact the personnel department *each* day of your illness.	Warning	3 days off	Discharge	
8. Excessive absenteeism—5 days within any 90 consecutive working days.	Warning	Discharge		
9. Three consecutive working days of ununreported absence.	Discharge			
10. Four days (not consecutive) of unreported absence within any one-year period.	Discharge			
11. Fighting and/or horseplay on company premises.	Discharge			
12. Drinking of alcoholic beverage during working hours.	Discharge			

EXHIBIT 5–7 (*continued*)

Rules	*Penalties*			
	First offense	*Second offense*	*Third offense*	*Fourth offense*
13. Reporting to work under the influence of alcohol.	Discharge			
14. Insubordination	Discharge			
15. Unauthorized possession of firearms and/or weapons.	Discharge			
16. Leaving your work area without permission.	Warning	3 days off	5 days off	Discharge
17. Leaving plant during working hours without permission.	Discharge			
18. Receiving personal telephone calls.	Warning	3 days off	5 days off	Discharge
19. Placing personal telephone calls.	Warning	3 days off	5 days off	Discharge
20. Gambling on company property.	Discharge			
21. Sleeping on the job.	Discharge			

EXHIBIT 5–7 (*continued*)

	Penalties			
Rules	*First offense*	*Second offense*	*Third offense*	*Fourth offense*
22. Failure to observe designated parking areas.	Warning	3 days off	5 days off	Discharge
23. Deliberately destroying company property, including tools, equipment, machinery, and vehicles.	Discharge			
24. Loafing	Warning	3 days off	5 days off	Discharge
25. Failure to punch timecard in or out on time.	Warning	3 days off	5 days off	Discharge
26. Theft or removal from the premises without proper authorization any company or employee property.	Discharge			
27. Mistakes due to carelessness.	Warning	3 days off	5 days off	Discharge
28. Entering restricted area without permission.	Warning	Discharge		

EXHIBIT 5–7 (*continued*)

	Penalties			
Rules	*First offense*	*Second offense*	*Third offense*	*Fourth offense*
29. Soliciting contributions for any purpose unless approved by personnel department.	Warning	Discharge		
30. Immoral conduct.	Discharge			
31. Posting or removing any item from bulletin board without permission of personnel department.	Warning	Discharge		
32. Distribution of printed items on company property without permission of personnel department.	Warning	Discharge		
33. Threatening or intimidating any employee.	3 days off	Discharge		
34. Poor housekeeping.	Warning	3 days off	5 days off	Discharge
35. Contributing to unsanitary conditions.	Warning	3 days off	5 days off	Discharge

EXHIBIT 5–7 (*continued*)

	Penalties			
Rules	*First offense*	*Second offense*	*Third offense*	*Fourth offense*
36. Restricting or attempting to cause or convince others to restrict production.	Discharge			
37. Failure to report on "date of return" from leave of absence.	Discharge			
38. Failure to return when recalled from layoff.	Discharge			
39. Giving confidential company information to unauthorized personnel.	Discharge			
40. Performing unauthorized work on company time.	Discharge			
41. Unauthorized loitering before or after working hours.	Warning	3 days off	5 days off	Discharge

EXHIBIT 5–7 (*continued*)

Rules	Penalties			
	First offense	*Second offense*	*Third offense*	*Fourth offense*
42. Failure to report to personnel department an injury (to yourself or a fellow employee) on the day of such injury.	Discharge			
43. Failure of a female employee to notify personnel department that she is pregnant and obtain doctor's statement.	Discharge			
44. Personal use of company property.	Discharge			
45. Improperly using discount privileges.	Discharge			
46. Failure to observe designated dress regulations.	Warning	3 days off	5 days off	Discharge
47. Failure to give proper receipt to customers.	Discharge			

EXHIBIT 5–7 (*continued*)

	Penalties			
Rules	*First offense*	*Second offense*	*Third offense*	*Fourth offense*
48. Carelessness in using cash register.	Warning	3 days off	5 days off	Discharge
49. Discourtesy to customers.	Warning	3 days off	5 days off	Discharge
50. Failure to obey safety rules.	Discharge			
51. Distracting others through shouting, screaming, or demonstrations on company premises.	Discharge			
52. Making false or malicious statements concerning any employee or the company.	Discharge			
53. Abusive language to any employee or customer.	Discharge			
54. Fail to follow instructions.	5 days off	Discharge		

EXHIBIT 5–7 (*concluded*)

Rules	*Penalties*			
	First offense	*Second offense*	*Third offense*	*Fourth offense*

January 20, 1975. *Claimant John Simmons denied the fact that he was warned on January 8, 1975.* Because company A could not produce a copy of a warning letter, they lost their protest and Simmons collected over $3,000 from company A. That's quite a lot of money to pay just because the warning was not in writing! *The state unemployment agency expects you, the employer to keep good records—not the employee.*

EXHIBIT 5–8

Notice of disciplinary action

Name of employee ______________ Dept. ______________

Location ______________ Job title ______________

REASON FOR WARNING

( ) Excessive absenteeism
( ) Fighting
( ) Insubordination
( ) Timecard violation (explain below)
( ) Violation of dress code
( ) Theft
( ) Leaving area without permission
( ) Violation of safety rules
( ) Excessive tardiness
( ) Abusive language
( ) Sleeping on job
( ) Carelessness
( ) Other (explain) ______________

____

Reasons for action: ______________

____

____

( ) First warning
( ) Second warning
( ) Warning resulting in suspension for ____ working days, from ______ (date) through ______ (date).
( ) Additional warning will result in discharge

Signed and copy given to:

______________ Supervisor Date ______________

______________ Employee Date ______________

______________ Union steward Date ______________

______________ Other Date ______________

IMPORTANT. If, for some reason, you absolutely cannot give a warning in writing, that is, it must be verbal, have a witness present who can corroborate your testimony if need be. Mark your records indicating the date of the warning,

EXHIBIT 5–9

Notice of disciplinary action

Name of employee ____________________ Dept. ____________

Location ________________________ Job title ____________

Reason for disciplinary action: ____________________

Action taken:

( ) Warning ( ) Suspension—give dates

from (date) to (date)

Signatures:

____________________ Supervisor Date_____

____________________ Employee Date_____

____________________ Union steward Date_____

Copies to:

Supervisor	( )	Yes	( )	No	Date_____
Employee	( )	Yes	( )	No	Date_____
Union steward	( )	Yes	( )	No	Date_____

the reason for the warning, *the reaction of the employee being warned,* and who the witness was.

The following points about disciplinary action should be remembered:

1. Disciplinary action should not be too severe. The "punishment should fit the crime."

2. The warning should be given at the time the act occurs that is causing the warning.

   EXAMPLE. Susie Jones is absent without calling in on January 10. Her employer does not warn her until January 20. She should have been warned on January 11, when she reported for work.

3. If someone breaks a rule that normally carries a reprimand, and a reprimand is not given in this instance, you are, in effect, condoning the action, possibly without realizing it.

chapter

6

Separation procedures

The action and record keeping taken at the time of separation can determine the extent of your unemployment liability and the resulting charges. We will discuss proper record keeping when an employee voluntarily quits, how to properly discharge an employee who has committed misconduct, and some hints on reducing benefit charges when layoffs occur.

Discharge for misconduct

As we have previously discussed, in order to prove misconduct, you must prove:

1. You had a rule,
2. The employee knew about the rule, and
3. The employee broke the rule.

Assuming you can prove the above items through proper documentation, at the time a person commits the final act which causes his or her discharge, there are two cardinal rules to follow:

1. Discharge the employee when the act occurs that is causing the discharge.
2. Tell the employee the *real* reason for the discharge.

Let's discuss each of these items in detail. Remember, you may feel someone has been discharged for misconduct, but it must be proven. No matter how much you might feel that "misconduct" was committed, it must be proven as follows:

1. When an employee commits an act that is grounds for a misconduct discharge, discharge the employee when the act occurs that causes the discharge. For example, employee X has been warned about tardiness. X was told at the last warning that one more tardy within the following 30 days would mean a discharge; X comes to work an hour late today. *He or she should be discharged today—not tomorrow but today.*

   Should X file an unemployment claim, the state will always ask, "What happened on your last day?" If nothing happened, they will most likely rule that there was no misconduct.

   Too often, employers discharge someone at the employer's convenience, that is, normally, when a replacement is found. It may be necessary that you do this on occasion, but remember, you will then have little chance of proving misconduct and obtaining a disqualification.

   There are two extenuating circumstances which may preclude the immediate discharge of an employee and could still result in a disqualification should an unemployment claim be filed:

a. When the act occurs that should result in immediate discharge, there is no one at the location who has the authority to discharge an employee. This normally happens on a second or third shift, or night shift. An alternative to discharging the person would be to place the person on an immediate suspension. The employee could be told to leave work immediately and report at "such and such" time the following day. Actually, if you think about a suspension of this type, it is not such a bad idea, anyway. All the facts could be investigated; especially when heads are "cooler" and a more proper decision made.

b. A final act of misconduct occurs which no one knows about for some time. For example, suppose someone charges some personal expenses to your company. The matter is not discovered until 30–60 days later. If the employee is discharged as soon as this matter is discovered, you have, in effect, taken action immediately upon knowledge of the misconduct. Should an unemployment claim be filed, the state should be made aware that you took immediate action upon discovering the misconduct.

2. When an employee commits an act that is grounds for misconduct and is discharged when the act of misconduct is discovered, the employee must be told the *real* reason for the discharge.

For example, today you discharge employee X for excessive tardiness. You should remind X, at the time of discharge, about your previous warning that one more tardy within 30 days and you would discharge X. In accordance with your last warning, since X was tardy this morning you are, therefore, discharging X for excessive tardiness.

If an employment claim is filed, the state will ask the claimant, "What was said to you when you were discharged?" No matter how good a case you had prior to the discharge, no matter how well documented were your rules and warnings, the whole thing will be "for naught" if the employee is not told the act of misconduct that is causing the discharge. Oftentimes, the employer will take "the easy way out" by telling the employee that he or she is being discharged because the company is cutting back its staff, or laying off some employees—when, in fact, the employee is being discharged for misconduct. This seems to happen more so when a salaried person, rather than an hourly person is discharged.

CAUTION. Some employers do not really discharge employees—they lay them off because of lack of work and just don't recall them. The act of discharge never takes place. For a discharge to take place, you must tell someone he or she is being discharged.

CAUTION. If you have a probationary period for new employees, treat them (in re-

> spect to misconduct) as you would any other employees. These people can draw unemployment benefits just as anyone else. The tendency of most employers is to terminate probationary employees for "unsatisfactory work," rather than for the real cause, that is, misconduct. Many employers, by the terms of the labor agreement, do not have to indicate any reason for the discharge of a probationary employee. However, by not following our suggestions, you might pay unnecessarily for someone's benefits.[1]

Voluntary quit

In most states, a claimant will receive a disqualification if the claimant voluntarily quit without good cause, or without good cause attributable to the employer. "Without good cause attributable to the employer" means that it was not the employer's fault the claimant quit. "Attributable to the employer" relates not only to conditions of employment but also to the employer's conduct. Thus, if an employer continually harasses the claimant until the claimant quits, the claimant may be said to have quit "with good cause attributable to his or her employer" and will not be disqualified. The burden of proof is on the claimant to prove the contention that he or she quit with good cause attributable to the employer. If the claimant does not prove his or her contention, the claimant will be disqualified. The term "attributable to the

[1] See section on "Probationary Evaluation" in beginning of Chapter 5.

employer" is very important because in states where the regulation states "quit without good cause" and no mention is made of "attributable to the employer," all the claimant may have to prove to prevent a disqualification is that in the claimant's opinion, he or she had good cause to quit.

The word "voluntary" refers to "how" a leaving takes place. Someone may leave his or her work but may not do so voluntarily. Following are examples of involuntary leaving:

1. Employee X is told that either X must quit or X will be fired. So, X quits. Should X file for unemployment benefits, the state will rule X was discharged, and the employer will have to prove "misconduct" in order for a disqualification to result. In order to determine whether someone quit or was discharged, the state will normally try and determine "who approached whom first regarding the subsequent separation. If the employer approached the claimant first, no matter what the personnel records indicate, the separation was a discharge. A separation term heard frequently is "by mutual consent." The "who approached whom first" test would determine whether it was a quit or a discharge.
2. Employee D is discharged, but the employer tells D that the personnel records will be marked "voluntary quit" so that D's future work search will not be marred by a discharge. However, when D files for unem-

ployment benefits, the state determines D was discharged.

3. Employee L voluntarily quits due to illness or personal injury. This, on the surface, is an involuntary separation. After the illness or injury, L may file for unemployment benefits. If L did not ask for a leave of absence until such time as L or L's doctor expected that L could work again, L has, in effect, exercised a choice in terminating the employer-employee relationship. Therefore, you should protest the claim as a voluntary quit, and indicate L did not exercise L's rights to request a leave of absence. Of course, if L asked for a leave of absence and it was refused, and L quit, L has not left work voluntarily and will not be disqualified. L's separation is involuntary and non-disqualifying.

Most employers feel that for their protection, it is best to obtain a signed voluntary quit statement from an employee who is quitting. A simple form such as the one indicated in Exhibit 6–1 is satisfactory.

Many employers attempt to secure the employee's signature on a form of this type so that there can be no question about the fact the person actually quit. Of course, many people quit without notice. In these instances, you may not be able to obtain such a statement unless you tell the person he or she will not receive a final payroll check until he or she comes in to your office and signs a voluntary quit statement.

EXHIBIT 6–1

Voluntary quit statement

I voluntarily quit my employment with ___(Company)___ for the following reason(s): ____________________

____

____

My last day of employment will be ____________________

If you are quitting to move to another area, please indicate the locality ____________________.
If you are quitting to attend school, please indicate the school name ____________________.
If you are quitting to accept employment elsewhere, please indicate the name of your new employer ____________________.

Signed ____________________ Date ____________________

Lack of work layoffs

Most employers feel that when lack of work layoffs occur nothing can be done to control unemployment compensation charges. The thinking goes something like this:

> "Because of a cutback in production, we will have to lay off 30 employees. When they file for unemployment benefits, we will not protest any of the claims. Therefore, there is nothing we can do."

True, claims resulting from lack of work layoffs will not be protested. However, through a better understanding of who normally *does not* want unemployment benefits to be the primary source of income, and through certain separation procedures, unemployment benefit charges resulting from lack of work separations can be controlled.

Who are the people most likely to collect unemployment benefits? Generally speaking, those people who do not have to support themselves or dependents. Those who have to support themselves or dependents must find work quicker than those who do not have such obligations. There are exceptions, of course; but if the spouse is not working, the primary wage earner, it seems to us, would not want to be unemployed for any great length of time.

What other types of people generally do not draw unemployment benefits except when necessary?

1. Single (unmarried) individuals.
2. College students.
3. Those who have a history of working continuously.
4. Seemingly dedicated individuals.

We are not suggesting who you should hire, only stating that certain categories of individuals are more likely not to depend on unemployment benefits, except in an emergency.

Temporary work

When seeking employees who will be employed for only a set period of time, the following alternatives should be considered. Whether someone is being employed for one week, two weeks, or for the summer, if you terminate the employee because there is no work and the employee otherwise qualifies to collect unemployment benefits, your company, at sometime in the future, will have to pay at least a portion of the employee's unemployment benefits. Following are various alternatives to consider that can eliminate unemployment claims after temporary work is completed.

1. Employers, oftentimes, have an in-house labor pool, members of which can be used wherever needed. This eliminates the need for hiring extra employees on a temporary basis who will eventually be laid off and draw unemployment benefits. Other employers have an outside pool of individuals who do not want to work full time but want work on an as-needed basis. It may take several years to accumulate the individuals for the outside pool.
2. Use a temporary-help service. Many of them will even allow you to hire employees—but the temporary help service will pay them. This might be especially advantageous if you are going to hire a large number of employees on a temporary basis. All unemployment benefits will be charged to the temporary help company rather than to you. You will pay the temporary help company more per hour than you would pay directly to the employees; however, the unemployment charges resulting from a layoff would not affect your unemployment tax rate. Just ten people—each earning $500—could result in total unemployment charges of $1,600 to $5,000 (depending on the state). Because of the charges, your tax rate could increase, actually costing you more than the charges themselves. Many employers hire additional personnel prior to Christ-

mas, Valentine's Day, and prior to other holidays. The use of a temporary-help agency for payroll purposes at the time these additional employees are hired could result in less benefit charges and lower unemployment tax rates.

3. Schedule overtime for your regular employees rather than hire temporary employees. The regular employees would probably welcome the extra income, and no layoffs would occur when production level decreases. Overtime is expensive, but so is an increase in your unemployment tax rate due to layoffs.

Part-time work

You might, on occasion or permanently, need employees to work part time, that is, so many hours or days per week. See the alternatives already discussed in the above "Temporary Work" section. The same alternatives should be considered. In many instances, a person who works part time only wants to work part time *only*. In order to collect unemployment compensation, a person must be available for full-time permanent work. Therefore, an applicant who states that only part-time work is wanted should not collect unemployment benefits. However, the fact that the employee wants only part-time work should be well documented at the time of hire.

Temporary layoffs

Many employers have what is called a temporary layoff of some of their employees. These layoffs, due to decreases in production, shutdowns for maintenance purposes, or other reasons, usually last from a few days to several weeks. By planning the layoff properly, unemployment benefits can be substantially reduced. Following are various layoff procedures that can save enormous sums of money.

1. While a temporary layoff cannot be avoided, you can possibly save substantial sums of money if you will follow one simple procedure: Whenever possible, do not lay off your employees at the end of the shift on Friday or Saturday evening. Instead, lay them off at the end of the shift on Monday night, Tuesday night, Wednesday night, or Thursday night. Our reasoning is as follows:

   In order to determine how much money a person can collect in unemployment benefits, the state will *subtract* the person's earnings for that particular week from his or her weekly benefit amount. For example, employee A works on Monday and Tuesday and is laid off on Wednesday, Thursday, or Friday, and Monday and Tuesday of the following week A earns $30 per day. Therefore, working on Monday and Tuesday, A was paid $60. Suppose A's weekly benefit amount is $70:

	$70	weekly benefit amount
Less	60	earned on Monday and Tuesday
	$10	is what A will collect in unemployment benefits

   The following week, A is laid off on Monday and Tuesday, and works on Wednesday, Thursday, and Friday. At $30 per day, A would have earned $90:

	$70	weekly benefit amount
Less	90	earned on Wednesday, Thursday, and Friday
	$ 0	is what A could collect in unemployment benefits

A actually earned more than A's weekly benefit amount, and, therefore, cannot collect any unemployment benefits for this second week.

If company X had laid off A for one full calendar week (Monday to Monday), A would not have had any wages for that week and could have collected $70 in benefits. Company X saved $60 by laying off A from midweek to midweek rather than one full calendar week. Having 100 employees, company X, by following this procedure just once during the year, saved in excess of $6,000 ($60 × 100).

2. Stagger layoffs. Instead of laying off a complete department, lay off one person for two days during a week, lay off another person in that department for two days the following week, and so on. In this manner, no one will be laid off for an extended period of time, and no one will collect unemployment benefits.
3. If times are really bad, go to a four-day workweek for all employees (with their approval) so that no one will have to be laid off. With proper planning, a reduction in production and resultant layoffs do not have to result in mass unemployment benefits. Even realizing that layoffs are many times governed by union agreements, employers

oftentimes have more discretion of who to lay off and when to lay off than they realize.

Exit interview Normally, the exit interview is used as a tool in determining reasons people leave a company, as well as attitudes toward management and fellow employees. Little thought is given to the fact that the exit interview can be used to help reduce unemployment benefits charged to your company. If the exit interview is used to determine reasons people leave your company, and proper action is taken to correct improper supervision, low pay, inadequate training, or any other "correctable" reason for resignation, turnover will decrease, thereby creating less "possible" unemployment claims. Also, by determining reasons for leaving, perhaps hiring and indoctrination procedures can be strengthened, leading to less voluntary quits in the future. For example, suppose employee X tells you she is quitting because she can't type fast enough or correct enough to do her job properly. Your preemployment testing could be strengthened so that the "right" person is hired to fill a particular position.

A substantial reduction in turnover can have a drastic effect on the number of unemployment claims filed. Oftentimes, the personnel department of companies are responsible for policies that reduce turnover. However, results are generally measured in terms of more tangible savings, that is, reduced expenditures in such areas as recruiting, selection, training, and evaluation. Credit should also be given for a reduction in unemployment claims, thereby controlling un-

EXHIBIT 6–2

Exit interview letter

So that we can obtain your opinion of our company, our supervision, and our policies, we are asking that you complete the attached questionnaire.

Please feel free to criticize and/or make suggestions. Your replies will be held in strict confidence. If you so desire, you can omit the first section.

Your cooperation is appreciated.

employment benefit charges and reducing (or, at least controlling) unemployment tax rates. See Exhibits 6–2 and 6–3 for an example of an exit interview letter and form.

For anyone who gives notice that he or she is quitting, the form could be completed prior to or on the last day. For others, it could be mailed along with a stamped self-addressed envelope.

EXHIBIT 6–3

Exit interview

Name ______________________ Date ______________

Dates of employment: From ____________ To ____________

Location worked ____________ Department ____________

Position ______________ Salary or wage ____________

Please Answer and Explain

Why did you accept employment with us? ____________

____

At the time you were hired, was anything told to you, or implied, that was not true? Yes ______ No ______

____

____

EXHIBIT 6–3 (*continued*)

When you were hired, were you promised anything that you did not get? Yes ______ No ______

____

____

When you were hired, were your duties explained? Yes ______ No ______

____

____

When you were hired, were our rules of conduct given to you? Yes ______ No ______

____

____

Were you satisfied with your wages? Yes ______ No ______

____

____

Were you satisfied with the working conditions? Yes ______ No ______

____

____

Throughout your employment, were you satisfied with the position(s) you held? Yes ______ No ______

____

____

Do you have any skills or experience that you feel were not used? Yes ______ No ______

____

____

Did you receive recognition for "a job well done"? Yes ______ No ______

____

____

How would you classify yourself? (check one)

Dedicated ________
Industrious ________
Hard worker ________
Average worker ________
Work because I have to ________

EXHIBIT 6–3 (*continued*)

Do you feel the company has adequate employee benefits? Yes _______ No _______

____

____

Did your supervisor ever compliment you? Yes _______ No _______

____

____

Did your supervisor ever discipline you? Yes _______ No _______

____

____

Do you feel your supervisor delegated work to others? Yes _______ No _______ Did he or she delegate—

a. Too much work to others _______
b. Too little work to others _______

____

____

Were you kept informed of changes (products, personnel, or procedures) within the company? Yes _______ No _______

____

____

Did you ever make any suggestions? Yes _______ No _______ If "yes," were you contacted regarding the suggestions? Yes _______ No _______

____

____

If you voluntarily quit, how long have you considered quitting?

____

____

If you quit, for what reason did you quit? _______________

____

Would you work here again? Yes _______ No _______

____

____

Does your new position have:

Shorter hours. Yes _______ No _______

EXHIBIT 6–3 (*concluded*)

More pay. Yes ______ No ______
Better working conditions. Yes (explain) ______
No ______
More opportunity. Yes (explain) ______ No ______
Do you feel the top management is fair? Yes ______
No ______
____
____
Do you have any suggestions? Yes ______ No ______
____
____
Additional comments: ______________________________
____
____
____
____
____

Separation form

When a person is separated from your company, for whatever reason, you must keep complete records of the reason he or she no longer works for you. A person may not file a claim for as long as 18 months to 2 years after he or she leaves you, and you may still be liable for a portion of his or her benefits. It could cost you a full claim simply because an exact record of the reason for separation was not made at the time of his or her separation.

There are three requirements to good record keeping when someone is separated:

1. A good separation form must be available. We have provided you with several ex-

amples of these forms (see Exhibits 6–4 and 6–5). If your company uses a personnel action type form, be sure there are an adequate number of reasons for separation so that there will be no question regarding the reason the person no longer works for you.

2. The separation report should be completed by the person directly responsible for the separated employee. Who knows better the reason for termination than the supervisor? (The separation form could be completed by the personnel department, but should be done only after information regarding the reason for separation is received from the supervisor.)
3. The person who completes the separation form should give all details of the reason(s) for separation.

The termination form should be completed at the time of separation, not a week or a month later when facts are hazy. Every detail of the termination should be noted. If the person quit, why did he or she quit (if you know the reason). If the person was discharged, what incident or incidents led up to the discharge. Be specific. These incidents may have to be recalled a year later when the person files a claim. If necessary, you should have the supervisor complete another form rather than allow an incomplete form to be filed. Remember, when this person files a claim, the supervisor may have left your company. Without good records, you may have much difficulty in proving "misconduct."

EXHIBIT 6–4

Separation form

IMMEDIATELY UPON THE SEPARATION OF AN EMPLOYEE COMPLETE THIS FORM IN DUPLICATE AND DISTRIBUTE AS FOLLOWS:

Original—
Employer's name and address:
____
____
____
Employee's name __________
Address ________________
Soc. Sec. No. ______ Dept. ____
Position held ____________
Part time ( )
Full time ( )
Eligible for rehire ( )

Copy—
Unemployment account no. ___
First day worked ________
Last day worked ________
Date terminated ________
Rate of pay __________
If payment in lieu of notice was paid, give amount: $______
For period from ____ to ____
If vacation or severance pay was paid on or after last day worked, give amount: $____
for period from ____ to ____

VOLUNTARY QUIT

( ) To accept other work
( ) Never showed up or called after __________
( ) Failed to return from leave of absence
( ) No given reason
( ) Personal reasons (explain below)
( ) Voluntary retirement
( ) Dissatisfaction with job
( ) To attend school
( ) Change in residence
( ) To look for other employment
( ) Military service
( ) Retirement (explain below)
( ) Pregnancy
( ) Lost means of transportation
( ) Illness
( ) Home duties
( ) Other voluntary leaving

EXHIBIT 6–4 (*continued*)

DISCHARGE FOR MISCONDUCT (explain below)

( ) Refused to follow instructions
( ) Absenteeism
( ) Drinking on job (when, where)
( ) Dishonesty
( ) Broke company rule
( ) Falsified application form
( ) Discourtesy to customer
( ) Lateness
( ) Improper conduct
( ) Other misconduct

OTHER

( ) Laid off—lack of work
( ) Not qualified—discharged
( ) Labor dispute
( ) Mandatory retirement
( ) Presently on leave of absence
From ______________
To ______________
( ) Injury
( ) Refused work to start on ______________

Other details regarding termination: ______________________
____
____
____

Name ______________________
Date ______________________

EXHIBIT 6–5

Separation form

Name ______________________ Soc. Sec. No. ________________

Department ________________ Date of hire ________________

Position __________________ Last day worked _____________

Vacation pay: Amount $_____ from (date) to (date)

Termination pay: Amount $_____ from (date) to (date)

REASON FOR SEPARATION

VOLUNTARY QUIT

( ) Never showed up or called.
( ) Walked off the job.
( ) Sickness.
( ) Dissatisfaction with job.
( ) Moved.
( ) To look for other work.
( ) Other (explain below).

DISCHARGE (explain below)

( ) Lateness.
( ) Drinking.
( ) Did not follow instructions.
( ) Absenteeism.
( ) Broke rule.
( ) Other misconduct.

OTHER

( ) Lack of work.
( ) Not qualified.
( ) Injury.
( ) Refused work to start on __________

EXHIBIT 6–5 (*continued*)

Details: ______________________________

____

____

____

____

Date ______________ Signed ______________

chapter 7

Claims control

Many of the personnel policies discussed in several prior chapters have been leading to this chapter. If you have followed our recommended policies and a former employee files for unemployment benefits, by acting properly and quickly upon receipt of the claim form, the natural sequence of events will be: maximum control over your unemployment charges.

Organization and control

Your staff, and procedures, must be organized so that an unemployment claim form is processed immediately upon receipt.

SUGGESTIONS

1. *Assign the responsibility of processing unemployment claims to one person.* If you have more than one location, the responsibility can be delegated to one person at each location; *or* if the locations are very small regarding numbers of employees, you could direct one person at each location to send the claim notices, upon receipt, to an individual at the corporate office. Of course, in order for the latter procedure to be effec-

tive, proper separation (and in some instances, payroll) information must be maintained at the corporate office.

This consideration for a proper flow of claims forms within your organization must not be overlooked. For example, suppose you have a corporate headquarters, 2 plants, and 30 sales offices scattered throughout the United States. You might determine that the two plants should process their own unemployment claims. However, in all likelihood, the sales offices will not be staffed with personnel either with the experience or the inclination to handle unemployment claims. Therefore, the person who heads each sales office should be informed (and reinformed on a periodic basis) that any item received pertaining to unemployment compensation should be forwarded *on the day of receipt* to a certain individual at the corporate office. The sales office head should be told that failure to properly send a claim document could cost the company a very substantial amount of money, that is, the maximum cost of one claim in that particular state.

2. *Determine where (to what location) you want the state to mail the claim notices.*

Basically, there are two types of claim forms:

a. Base-period notices mailed to the official address of your company (see Exhibit 7–1 for definition of "base period").

b. Last employer (or renewed claim) notices mailed to the exact location where

EXHIBIT 7-1

Definitions

BASE PERIOD

The period of time prior to the filing of an unemployment claim used to determine:

1. Claimant's weekly benefit amount.
2. Claimant's maximum benefit amount.
3. Employers who are liable for claimant's unemployment benefits.

The base period of a claim is normally the first four of the last five completed calendar quarters. For example, suppose a claim is filed August 10, 1975:

	1975		1974		
8–10–75	*Second Quarter*	*First Quarter*	*Fourth Quarter*	*Third Quarter*	*Second Quarter*
•	Last five completed calendar quarters				
•		First four of the last five completed calendar quarters			
Third Quarter					

The base period, then, is the period April 1, 1974 through March 31, 1975. Every employer for whom the claimant worked during this period of time is potentially liable for the claimant's unemployment benefits *and will receive a base-period claim notice*, sometimes called an initial claim form, or a new claim form.

Variations. Some states have a base period of the 52-week period *prior* to the filing of the claim, while some use the first 4 of the last 6 completed calendar quarters, while still a few others use the last 4 completed calendar quarters.

Suggestion. It is not important that you determine the base period of every initial claim form or base-period notice you receive. What is important is that you realize that someone could have worked for you five or six quarters prior to the filing of the claim and you are still liable. Thus, we emphasize keeping good employee personnel records—both during a person's employment and at the time of a person's termination. Most states mail the base-period

EXHIBIT 7-1 (*continued*)

notice to the official mailing address of a company, rather than to the location where the person actually worked.

BENEFIT YEAR

The 365-day period from the filing date of the new claim to the same date one year later. For example, a claim filed on August 10, 1975 would have a benefit year from August 10, 1975 to August 9, 1976.

As previously discussed, the base-period notice is mailed to base-period employers. Only one new claim per benefit year can be filed. All other claims filed after the benefit year begins are called renewed claims. The claim forms mailed when a renewed claim is filed are normally mailed to the location where the person worked, rather than to the official mailing address. During the complete benefit year, no matter how many renewed claims are filed, the base period does not change.

the person worked. This form is mailed to the location at which the claimant worked because a clerk at the local state unemployment office asks the person where he or she worked and the "last employer" or "renewed" claim notice is mailed to that location.

If you so desire, you may write the state unemployment agency and ask them to mail all base-period notices to one particular address within or outside of the state. There are just a few states that will not comply with this request.

CAUTION. Remember, only the *base-period* claim notices can be directed to wherever you so desire. Therefore, using our example cited above, regarding the company that has 30 sales offices, after your request is made to have base-period notices mailed to the corporate headquarters, you must still inform the appropriate people at the 30 locations that they should forward claims data to the corporate office. In other words, don't think that because you made the request to have the base-period notices mailed to a particular address that certain claim forms and other claims media will not be received at the locations. Also, the state could err and send a base-period notice to an incorrect address. Of course, the reverse situation could occur. All of the base-period notices might be going to your home office rather than to the plant facilities. If you want them to go to the plant facilities, write to the state agency and ask them how this can be accomplished. Most states will give each facility a separate "unit," "establishment," or "location" number, and mark their records with the address of each so that claim forms will be mailed to the location. You might want to consider this procedure even if you want all claim forms to be mailed to the corporate office. By establishing a separate unit number for each location in a state within a given corporation, most states will separate benefit charges so that charges can be allocated to particular locations, or so that the charge statements themselves can be mailed to the location where the person worked to be verified or reviewed by the personnel from that location.

3. *Consider keeping employee personnel records according to social security number rather than by name.* Much time can be lost looking for a name rather than a social security number. A person can change his or her name; however, a social security number cannot be changed.

   SUGGESTION. If you receive an unemployment claim form and cannot find that name in your file, write the unemployment agency, within the time limit for protesting, and tell them you have no record that the individual worked for you. Ask:

   a. The dates of employment, and
   b. If the person changed his name.

4. *Learn from the state unemployment agency.* Write for booklets they give to employers and claimants. Stop in at an unemployment office and talk with an employee. You may feel you don't want to spend the time, but it will be time well spent. If you have locations in many states, read the material you receive from the state. The people working at the state unemployment agency are always cooperative and willing to explain the regulations to an employer.

5. *Keep records of claims activity.* Whether you have one location or many locations processing claims, obtain activity reports from each of them. Otherwise, you will not know if claims were protested and whether the protests were won, lost, or pending. See Exhibit 7–2 for an example of such a reporting form. Such a report should be received on a periodic basis, that is, quarterly, or whatever.

   SUGGESTION. A report, such as the one in Exhibit 7–2, should be completed even if no unemployment claims or determinations were received. This will verify that none were, in fact, received.

EXHIBIT 7–2

Unemployment claims activity report

Location ______________________________

To be completed 4/1, 7/1, 10/1, and 1/1

Number of claims received last three months ____________

Unprotestable ____________

Protests made

Number won ____________________

Number lost ____________________

Decisions not received ____________

Attach copy of protests lost.

Signed ______________________________ Date ____________________

Claims protesting

Now that the general subject of claims has been discussed, the following section will cover the actual day-to-day handling of the claim forms. Following are several brief suggestions:

1. *All claim forms received should be processed in the same manner—whether they are base-period notices, renewed claim forms, or last employer notices.* Too often, an employer protests base-period notices but does not protest renewed or last employer notices. When *any* claim notice is received, if the claimant quit, was discharged for misconduct, or refused a work offer, a protest should be made, *even if you are not in the base period.* In many states, failure to protest will result in a loss of future protest rights.
2. *Read the claim notice and protest on time.* Annually, employers lose tens of thousands of dollars simply because they did not protest claims within the prescribed time limits.

   CAUTION. If you protest a claim within a day or two prior to the deadline, do not use your company postage-meter. If the protest arrives late, the state may use the date received rather than the postmark date when determining whether the protest was on time. Many companies keep a supply of postage stamps handy so that envelopes containing protests will be canceled by the U.S. Postal Service.

3. *Be sure claims are processed during vacations and/or plant shutdowns.* If the person who normally handles claims matters goes

on a two-week vacation, someone else should bear this responsibility while he or she is gone. If you have a periodic plant shutdown during the summer, at Christmas, or at any other time, someone should be responsible for coming in for at least a few hours to protest claims. Just suppose your company has a one-week plant shutdown and only two claims are not protested. If each of those claimants could draw $70 per week for 26 weeks, you would have needlessly lost $3,640 ($70 × 26 × 2).

4. *Be short, concise, and clear when protesting.* Give the facts, but don't overstate them or give a two-page explanation of what happened when one sentence would suffice.

Some rules of thumb when protesting are given in the following sections.

Protest properly

See Exhibits 7–3 through 7–8 for several examples of protest letters. Some states provide for space on certain claim forms to protest. However, other claim forms, such as last employer notices, may require a letter when a protest is made. When you examine them, you will notice that they are brief and to the point. You will also notice they are expressed in terms easy to understand. There is nothing difficult about protesting unemployment claims.

Voluntary quit

Just keep in mind that in order for you to win the protest, you must normally show that the claimant voluntarily quit for reasons attributable to conditions outside his or her employment with you. The following discussion is intended as a guideline rather than a rigid discussion of

EXHIBIT 7–3

Protest—voluntary quit

Division of Employment Security
(address where claim filed)

Re: Claimant: Wilmer Jones
Soc. Sec. No.: 483–75–4807
Account No.: 75285

GENTLEMEN:

We wish to protest the claim filed by the above claimant, because claimant has been separated for reasons other than lack of work.

Claimant voluntarily quit for the following reason:

Did not show up or call after . . 8–7–75
Last day worked 8–1–75
Position . . . . Driver
Rate of pay . . . . $3.75 per hr.

We formally request a determination as to the disposition of this claim. May we thank you in advance for your cooperation in this matter.

Very truly yours,
SMITH & JONES, INC.

John Apple
Personnel Manager

when you might win or lose protests. In most states, you will normally *win* your protest if a person voluntarily quit for the following reasons:

1. To accept other work. (Person may not be disqualified because many state unemployment agencies feel a person should not be penalized for trying to better oneself.

EXHIBIT 7–4
Protest—discharge for misconduct

Division of Employment Security
(address where claim filed)

Re: Claimant: Wilmer Jones
Soc. Sec. No.: 483–75–4807
Account No.: 72585

GENTLEMEN:

We wish to protest the claim filed by the above claimant, because claimant has been separated for reasons other than lack of work. Claimant was discharged for misconduct connected with employment.

He was tardy 10 times in his last month of employment and was warned in writing on 8/3/71.

Last day worked:	8–7–75	*Position:*	Clerk
Date terminated:	8–7–75	*Rate of pay:*	$3 per hr.

We formally request a determination as to the disposition of this claim. May we thank you in advance for your cooperation in this matter.

Very truly yours,
SMITH & JONES, INC.

John Apple
Personnel Manager

In some states, even though a person may not be disqualified, the employer is *not* charged for his or her unemployment benefits. Check the regulations in the states in which you have employees.)

2. To look for other employment.
3. Change in residence. (If one spouse quits to accompany the other spouse to another

EXHIBIT 7–5
Protest—labor dispute

Division of Employment Security
(Central Unemployment Office
cc: Local Unemployment Office)

Re: Claimant: Jack Jones
Soc. Sec. No.: 210–78–1432
Account No.: 75285

GENTLEMEN:

Following is a listing of all employees participating in a labor dispute which began at 12:01 A.M. on July 1, 1975. The last day worked was June 30, 1975.

Name	*Soc. Sec. No.*

Signed ______________________ Date ____________

locality because of work, the penalty for this type of voluntary quit is sometimes not as severe.)

4. To attend school.
5. Dissatisfaction with job (unless a person can show there was a good reason to be dissatisfied).
6. Personal reasons.

EXHIBIT 7–6

Protest—labor dispute (*refusal to cross picket line*)

Division of Employment Security
(address where claim filed)

Re: Claimant: John Storey
Soc. Sec. No.: 473–05–4170
Account No.: 75285

GENTLEMEN:

We wish to protest this claim filed by the above claimant. Claimant has refused to cross picket line of (union name).

Last day worked: 7–3–75
Position: Dock hand

We formally request a determination as to the disposition of this claim. May we thank you in advance for your cooperation in this matter.

Very truly yours,
SMITH & JONES, INC.

John Apple
Personnel Manager

7. To get married.
8. Home duties.
9. Voluntary retirement.
10. Lost transportation (in most states).
11. Several days of unreported absence.
12. Failure to return from a leave of absence.
13. Pregnancy.
14. No reason given.

In most states you will normally *lose* your protest if a person voluntarily quit for the following reasons:

EXHIBIT 7–7
Protest—leave of absence

Division of Employment Security
(address where claim filed)

Re: Claimant: Joyce Black
Soc. Sec. No.: 510–73–1470
Account No.: 75285

GENTLEMEN:

We wish to protest the claim filed by the above claimant, because claimant is presently on a maternity leave of absence from 8–10–75 to 12–5–75, granted at her request. We formally request a determination as to the disposition of this claim. May we thank you in advance for your cooperation in this matter.

Very truly yours,
SMITH & JONES, INC.

John Apple
Personnel Manager

1. Illness. (Normally, claimant must produce doctor's statement indicating the claimant had to quit employment because of medical reasons. To qualify to collect unemployment benefits, another doctor's statement must be provided stating the claimant's medical condition has improved enough for him or her to work. *If the claimant did not return to your company to seek work, you should protest the claim form stating this fact.* However, remember, the claimant, due to a physical condition, may not be able to return to his or her former occupation or

EXHIBIT 7–8
Protest—not available for work

Division of Employment Security
(address where claim filed)

Re:	Claimant:	Donna White
	Soc. Sec. No.:	843–50–7153
	Account No.:	75285

GENTLEMEN:

We wish to protest the claim filed by the above claimant, because we don't believe claimant is available for work. On 8–15–71, claimant was injured on the job and it is our understanding she is not able to work.

Last day worked: 8–15–75 *Position:* File clerk
Rate of pay: $2.30 per hr.

We formally request a determination as to the disposition of this claim. May we thank you in advance for your cooperation in this matter.

Very truly yours,
SMITH & JONES, INC.

John Apple
Personnel Manager

skill. In this event, if you do not have other work for the claimant to do, he or she will be eligible for unemployment benefits.)

2. Supervisor harassed the claimant.
3. Working conditions unbearable. For example, no ventilation in a plant.
4. Hours of work drastically reduced.
5. Promises made at the time of hire not fulfilled.

6. Forceable quit. If a person is told to quit or he or she will be discharged, this is, in effect, a discharge. (See Chapter 6.)
7. Impending layoff. A person quits to look for, or accept, other work when it is known (the person has been told) he or she is going to be laid off because of a lack of work. (In some states, a person may not be disqualified, but in other states, there might be disqualification for quitting in anticipation of a layoff. One important consideration is if a person "suspected" or was "told" he or she was going to be laid off. In any event, if the person voluntarily quit, the claim should be protested.)

Discharge for misconduct

You will normally *win* your protest if a person was discharged for the following reasons:

1. Company rule or policy broken (if you can prove claimant was aware of such rule or policy).
2. Drinking on the job.
3. Fighting on the job.
4. Stealing from you.
5. Refusal to follow instructions.
6. Insubordination.
7. Dishonesty (if proven).
8. Unexcused or unreported absenteeism (if warned).
9. Excessive tardiness (if warned).

You will normally *lose* your protest if a person was discharged for the following reasons:

1. Layoff because of a lack of work.
2. Pregnancy.

3. Unsatisfactory work.
4. Retirement.
5. Absenteeism, if properly reported. (The term "absenteeism" can be very ambiguous and, as discussed in a previous chapter, must be defined in terms of "excessive," "unreported," and so on. Normally, if a person is absent due to illness, reports the absences properly, and is discharged, it is very difficult to win a protest. Consider the following when protesting:
   a. Did the absences follow a pattern, that is, absent the day after payday, absent usually on Mondays, and so on?
   b. Do you have a rule defining excessive absenteeism? Was the employee aware of such a rule, and was he or she warned?
6. Tardiness (unless habitual and warned).

Labor dispute

A labor dispute is not really a termination. The person is still employed by you but may refuse to work. Normally, when a labor dispute starts, you should mail a listing to the state of those people who are participating in the labor dispute. See Exhibit 7–5. See Exhibit 7–6 for protest of a person who would not cross the picket line.

Leave of absence

A person on a leave of absence has not been separated; however, someone on a leave of absence might file for unemployment benefits. Please remember our previous suggestion that all leaves of absence be requested by the employee and in the employee's writing. See Exhibit 7–7, "Protest—Leave of Absence."

Eligibility

In just about every state, in order for someone to collect unemployment benefits, the claimant must be—

1. Able to work,
2. Available for work, and
3. Actively and earnestly seeking work.

The burden of proving eligibility normally is on the shoulders of the claimant. However, the burden is usually on the employer to bring to the attention of the state a situation that might cause the claimant to be ineligible. If you suspect the claimant is ineligible for any of the following reasons, either at the time the claim notice is received or anytime thereafter, a letter should be mailed to the unemployment agency:

1. Refusal of a suitable and bona fide work offer—see the section "Refusal to Accept Employment" later in this chapter.
2. Hours of work and/or days of work restricted.
3. Health not excellent—see Exhibit 7–8.
4. Final stages of pregnancy.
5. Not actively seeking work.
6. Does not want to work.
7. Lost transportation.
8. Is attending school.
9. Looks for work only occasionally.
10. Lost a babysitter.
11. Wants too much money to work.
12. Looks for work only in the locality in which he lives.
13. Is self-employed.

SUGGESTION. If possible, make a work offer at the time a claim form is received. If the claimant refuses the offer, send a letter to the claimant (certified, return-receipt requested) confirming the fact that the work offer was refused, with a copy to the state unemployment agency—see next section.

Refusal to accept employment

A claimant who refuses a bona fide work offer should be held ineligible from collecting unemployment compensation benefits. However, benefits are needlessly charged to employers, because employers, many times, do not keep adequate records, do not recall those who should be recalled, and do not promptly notify the state when a work offer is refused.

Employers generally feel that someone laid off because of lack of work should collect unemployment benefits, but that someone who refuses a bona fide work offer should be disqualified. Employers and state unemployment compensation are bilked of tens of thousands of dollars yearly because employers do not follow the procedures we are going to discuss.

When discussing refusal to accept reemployment, we are not concerned only with those employees who have been *laid off* who refuse recall, but (in several states) we also are concerned with recalling those employees who have voluntarily quit and are eligible for rehire. In the states of Illinois, Indiana, Iowa, Louisiana, Maryland, Michigan, Nevada, New Jersey, New York, North Dakota, Utah, and the District of Columbia, the employer can be charged for a person's unemployment benefits *after* an initial period of disqualification—even when that person voluntarily quit. The only recourse the employer has is to make a work offer. If the claimant refuses a bonified work offer and the state unemployment agency is properly and promptly notified, a disqualification should result. The following procedures should result in an efficient method for keeping proper records and reducing unemployment benefits resulting from former employees who refuse reemployment. Even if your laid-off employees are recalled in order of seniority, please keep in mind that the following discussion also involves recalling (hourly, but most likely salaried) employees who voluntarily quit in the states mentioned above.

1. Keep a record of those employees who have filed for unemployment benefits who have been laid off because of lack of work (or who quit in the states mentioned), and who are eligible for rehire. See Exhibit 7–9 for such a record-keeping form.
2. When a position is available for which any of the people who are listed are qualified, a work offer should be made; preferably to those people who earned the most wages. Your unemployment liability is directly proportionate to the claimant's earnings, that is, the more a person earned, the greater is your liability. Therefore, try and recall the person who earned the most money in the five quarters preceding his or her claim. If the person returns to work, he or she will

EXHIBIT 7–9

Former employees eligible for reemployment who have filed for unemployment benefits

Name	*Soc. Sec. No.*	*Wages earned in previous 5 quarters **	*If not lack of work, reason for separation †*	*Supervisor*

* Recall claimants whose earnings were greatest. The more a person earned, the greater your liability.

† Applies only to states which, even if the claimant quit, may eventually charge the employer; that is, Illinois, Indiana, Iowa, Louisiana, Maryland, Michigan, Nevada, New Jersey, New York, North Dakota, Utah, and the District of Columbia.

no longer draw unemployment benefits; if the person refuses the work offer and is subsequently disqualified, you may incur no further liability for his or her benefits.

3. Most employers desire to make a work offer in writing (see Exhibit 7–10); however, contacting the claimant by telephone has

EXHIBIT 7–10

Certified mail—return receipt requested

NOTICE OF WRITTEN WORK OFFER

To: ______________________ *Date:* ______________________
______________________ Soc. Sec. No.: ______________
____

The following position is available:
Location: ______________ Department: ______________
Classification: ______________ Rate of pay: ______________
Date to report: ______________
Time to report: ______________
Report to: ______________

Information regarding your last period of employment with us:
Location: ______________ Department: ______________
Classification: ______________ Rate of pay: ______________
Last day worked: ______________
Reason for separation: ______________________________

(If applicable)
Copy to: State Unemployment Office

Signed ______________________
Title ______________________

one distinct advantage—if the work offer is refused, you will most likely be able to find out the reason for the refusal, which is important. It is doubtful that the reason for the refusal can be obtained when the offer is made in writing. If a telephone call is made, a record of the conversation must be kept.

EXHIBIT 7–11

Telephone work offer

Name: ____________ Location of position: ____________
Soc. Sec. No. ____________ Department: ____________
Telephone no. ____________ Classification: ____________
Date of call: ____________ Rate of pay: ____________
Person spoken to: ____________ Date to report: ____________
Time to report: ____________
Report to: ____________

Accepted ____________
Refused ____________

If refused, reason: ____________

If accepted, confirmation letter sent on ____________ (date)
(copy attached)

If refused, confirmation letter sent on ____________ (date)
(copy attached)

Signed ____________ Date ____________

See Exhibit 7–11 for an example of such a record.

4. If the work offer is accepted, a letter of confirmation, such as the example on Exhibit 7–12, should be mailed to the claimant indicating the pertinent facts. Many employers do not send a letter of confirmation if the position is accepted; however, the claim-

EXHIBIT 7–12

Confirmation letter—position accepted

Name: ____________________ Date: ____________________

Address: ____________________ Soc. Sec. No.:

____________________ ____________________

Dear ____________________:

On ___(date)___ at ___(time)___, you spoke with ______(name)______ and accepted the following position:

Location: ____________________
Department: ____________________
Classification: ____________________
Rate of pay: ____________________
Date to report: ____________________
Time to report: ____________________
Report to: ____________________

We are happy that you accepted our offer and look forward to seeing you.

Signed: ____________________

Blind copy to:
State Unemployment Office
(attach copy to telephone work offer form)

ant may not report on the day he said he would report. A copy of the confirmation letter should be sent to the state unemployment office so they will be properly notified in the event the claimant does not return. Note the date the confirmation letter was sent on the telephone work offer form, and attach a copy to it.

5. If the work offer is refused, a confirmation letter should be sent by certified mail, return receipt requested, to the claimant. A copy should be sent to the unemployment office where the claim was filed. *This confirmation should be sent on the day the work offer is refused.* Many states have a time limit for notifying them of a work refusal. Failure to notify them on time could result in excess charges to your unemployment account. See Exhibit 7–13 for an example of a confirmation letter to be sent if a work offer is refused. Note the date the confirmation letter was sent on the telephone work offer form (Exhibit 7–11) and attach a copy to it.

In order to test whether a work offer is "reasonable" and "bona fide," the state will normally examine:

1. The position being offered. Is the claimant qualified to do the work? Has the claimant had experience doing that type of work?
2. The rate of pay. Is the rate of pay at least close to what the claimant was earning previously?

Each work offer is judged on its own merits. Of course, if you are dissatisfied with the state's decision after you are notified of a work refusal, you can appeal and ask for a hearing.

REMEMBER. The employer must take the initiative in notifying the state of either the acceptance or refusal of a work offer, and no

EXHIBIT 7–13

Certified mail, return receipt requested, confirmation letter—work offer refused

Name: ____________________ Date: ____________________
Address: ____________________ Soc. Sec. No.: ____________________
____________________ ____________________

Dear ______________:

We regret that you were not able to accept our work offer.

Information regarding your last period of employment with us:

Location: ______________ Department: ______________
Classification: ______________ Rate of pay: ______________
Last day worked: ______________ Reason for separation: ______________

The following work offer was made to you:

Location: ______________ Department: ______________
Classification: ______________ Rate of pay: ______________
Date to report: ______________ Time to report: ______________

______(name)______ spoke with you on ____(date)____ at ___(time)___ and you indicated you could not return for the following reason: ______________________________
____

Signed: ______________

Blind copy to:
State Unemployment Office
(attach copy to telephone work offer form)

matter what the penalty on a claimant for a work refusal, the state should be notified. Suppose someone told you he or she could not return to work for six months. After you notify the state of this fact, they might rule the claimant is not in the labor market and is ineligible for six months.

Extra remuneration

Most employers will give separated employees one or all of the following types of extra remuneration:

1. Severance pay.
2. Accrued vacation pay.
3. Retirement benefits.
4. Holiday pay (if on short-term layoff).

Each of these types of extra pay might be treated as wages (for purposes of unemployment benefits) and cause the claimant to be ineligible for the period of time for which it is allocated. The regulations in each state can be different; however, the following generalities should be considered. Many employers overlook the extra pay paid to employees upon termination, and as a result do not notify the state unemployment agency and lose countless thousands of dollars annually.

These types of extra payments will not have the same effect that a disqualification for, say, a voluntary quit would have. A voluntary quit might result in a disqualification of six weeks, and your account might then not be charged for benefits drawn by the claimant. By properly reporting these payments to the state unemployment agency, benefits paid to the claimant would either be delayed (i.e., severance pay and accrued vacation pay) or reduced (i.e., retirement benefits or holiday pay). However, don't underestimate the savings that could result. For example, if F. G. is given two weeks of accrued vacation pay at the time F. G. quits, files for unemployment benefits immediately, and finds employment after being out of work four (4) weeks, you could save two (2) full weeks of unemployment charges by following our suggestions.

Severance pay

Severance pay, paid to an employee who has been discharged is treated by some unemployment agencies as wages earned for the period of time it covers. In these states, if such payments are made to the employee, he or she cannot collect unemployment benefits for that period of time.

EXAMPLE. Employee X is discharged on 9/30 and is paid two weeks of severance pay. X could not collect unemployment benefits for this two-week period because the state unemployment agency would, in effect, treat the severance pay as wages.

All employers who have occasion to pay *severance* pay should check with the state unemployment agency in the states in which they are located in order to determine if such payments would cause a person to be ineligible for the covered period of time.

CAUTION. The terminology the employer uses for such severance payments can make the difference between someone collecting benefits and not collecting benefits. Commonly used terms for severance payments are:

1. Separation pay.
2. Severance pay.
3. Payment in lieu of notice.
4. Termination pay.

In Michigan, the employer should use the term "payment in lieu of notice" *and* should tell the separated employee the payments will be allocated over a certain period of time. The former employee will then not be able to collect unemployment benefits for the period of time the payments cover. Otherwise calling such payments "severance pay," for example, will have no effect whatsoever on the unemployment benefits.

SUGGESTION. Contact the unemployment agency to determine their policy toward separation pay; especially proper terminology and allocation of such payments. Then, formulate, or change, your company policy. When an unemployment claim form is received, determine if that person received severance pay (or payment in lieu of notice, and so on). If so, indicate to the state the amount of such payment and the period of time covered—for example, $200 for the period 10–1 through 10–14.

Accrued vacation pay

Accrued vacation pay is oftentimes given to separated employees.

EXAMPLE. Employee W quits on 9–30 but has earned two weeks of vacation time and has taken only one week of vacation. W earns $150 per week. At the time of W's separation, employer X gives W $150 for the unused week of vacation.

Many states will deny this claimant benefits for the week following separation because the claimant was given the $150 for one week of unused vacation time. If this is true in the state (or states) in which you have locations, you must notify the state at the time the claim notice is received—for example, "W received $150 of vacation pay to cover the period 10–1 through 10–7."

In the example cited, this notification could have saved you $150.

SUGGESTION. If you give accrued vacation pay at the time of separation, contact the state agency and determine the proper reporting procedure (to the state) when an unemployment claim is filed. Then, follow through when an unemployment claim form is received.

Plant shutdowns for vacation

Many employers close their plants at certain times of the year for vacations. Some employees, especially those who have not worked for the employer long enough to receive vacation pay, file for unemployment benefits. They have, in effect, been laid off—unless the union agreement states the plant *must* close for vacations on certain dates during the year.

SUGGESTION. Determine from your union contract(s) whether the agreement states the plant *must* shut down (bilateral agreement). If the wording is vague, or says nothing at all about a plant shutdown, most state unemployment agencies feel that your decision to close the plant for vacations is a unilateral agreement, that is, a one-sided agreement, decided on by management.

If the agreement states the plant must close, the employee, by joining the union, has agreed to this policy. Therefore, all unemployment claims received from such union members should be protested.

SUGGESTION. Perhaps work could be offered to those employees who either do not have vacation time coming, or those who do not have enough vacation time coming to receive vacation pay for the complete number of weeks the plant will be closed. If the work offer is refused, the unemployment agency could be notified when a claim notice is received.

Retirement benefits

At least a portion of monthly pension payments received by a former employee is usually deductible from unemployment benefits. Some states ask the former employer on the claim notice whether the claimant is receiving a pension, the amount of pension received per month, and what percentage the employer (or employee) contributed into the pension fund. All, or some, of these factors can be important.

If your company has a mandatory retirement plan, the pension deduction takes on added significance because someone who is forced to retire has actually been discharged, but not for misconduct, and will be eligible for unemployment benefits if the other requirements are met. However, the pension amount received might be great enough to keep the person from collecting unemployment benefits.

SUGGESTION. When an unemployment claim form is received for someone who was *forced* to retire, notify the state of—

1. The monthly dollar amount of pension the person is receiving.

2. The percentage of funds contributed into the fund by the employer.

If applicable in that state, a proportion of the monthly pension received will be subtracted from the person's unemployment benefits.

Holiday pay

During temporary layoffs, employers sometime give laid-off employees holiday pay. This happens most frequently during the Fourth of July, Christmas, and New Year's holidays. Normally, a person's unemployment benefits for the week in which a holiday occurs will be reduced by the amount of holiday pay the person received.

SUGGESTION. If you receive a lack of work claim for someone who received holiday pay for the week in which the person is claiming benefits, notify the state within the protest time period.

Claim determinations

After protesting a claim, you will, in most cases, be notified that you won or lost the protest (you will normally not be notified of anything if the claimant files a claim but never returns to collect benefits). You are probably saying right now, "How do I know if I've won or lost?"

When you receive a determination, *read it.* Generally speaking, if the claimant was disqualified for a certain number of weeks, or must find work and earn additional wages before the claimant can collect benefits, you have won. If the claimant is not disqualified, you have lost. If you are not sure of the outcome, call or write the person at the state who made the decision (the name is usually on the determination form).

Your objective in protesting is to stop your account from being charged for unemployment benefits. In some states, a disqualification means you should never be charged. In other states, a disqualification means benefits are delayed for a certain number of weeks, but eventually you will be charged should the claimant receive benefits.

Determination wins

If you have won your protest, file the determination. However, keep a separate record of this "win" so that you will have a ready reference in order to check future charge statements from the state. (See Chapter 8, "Verification of Benefit Charges.")

Determination loss

If you lost a protest you feel you should have won, write an appeal. Remember, the claims deputy or examiner who decided against you (or perhaps better stated, ruled for the claimant) is only human. The deputy's decision was based on your letter and statements made by the claimant. Perhaps the deputy didn't have all the facts. Or, perhaps your protest letter was not complete.

We live in a society that encourages protests and appeals. Use your rights. Also, keep in mind how much it will cost you if the claimant draws benefits from your account. Many employers state, "I don't want to spend the money it would cost to appeal. I will have to go to a hearing, and my time is too valuable." One claim might cost you over $3,000. We don't know how valuable your time is (you probably won't be the one that goes to the hearing anyway), but for an hour or two spent at the hearing, you might possibly save over $3,000. You will know you did your utmost to try and save your company money.

Caution. In some states, the appealing party must first ask for a redetermination prior to asking for a hearing before a referee. The state of Michigan has such a regulation. In Michigan, after receiving the original determination, you must ask for a redetermination. The redetermination decision can then be appealed, and a hearing will be held before a referee.

Please see Exhibit 7–14 for a sample appeal letter. Appeal letters should be brief. Write to the office where the determination was made and

EXHIBIT 7–14
Appeal letter

Date ____________________

Employment Security Division
1042 Main Street
Anytown, U.S.A.

Re: Harriet Smith
Soc. Sec. No. 123–45–6789

Gentlemen:

We would like to appeal the Claims Examiner's decision dated 10–1–75, because we believe claimant was discharged for misconduct connected with her work.

A hearing is respectfully requested.

Thank you.

Very truly yours,
Smith & Jones, Inc.

state that you would like to appeal the determination. A hearing will be set, and you will be notified, in writing, of the date and time.

Referee hearings

As discussed in the previous chapter, a referee hearing can result from the employer's appeal from a claim determination. However, hearings can also result, of course, from a claimant's appeal. The referee hearing is a more-or-less informal discussion between a referee, the claimant, and the employer. The referee wants to get at the truth regarding what happened, that is, was the claimant discharged for misconduct connected with his or her work, did the claimant have good cause to quit, was a bona fide work offer refused, and so on. The hearing usually takes place in a small room large enough for a table and several chairs. Even though the witnesses are "sworn in," a hearing is not like a court trial. Many employers, and especially supervisors, hesitate to request a hearing (or go to a hearing) simply because they are apprehensive about what is going to take place. Normally, the hearing itself takes about 30 minutes. Failure to ask for, or attend, a hearing could cost your company a full claim, possibly several thousand dollars.

Preparation

Bring with you to the hearing the claimant's personnel file indicating the first day worked, last day worked, rate of pay, position, and so on. If the claimant was warned, bring an extra copy of the written warning. If the claimant broke a company rule, bring an extra copy of that rule. If someone saw the claimant drinking, bring that person as a witness. If the claimant broke a rule in violation of a union contract, bring the union contract to turn in as evidence.

The most important person at the hearing should be the person who was closest to, or has the most knowledge about, the separation. For example, if the claimant was discharged by a supervisor, this supervisor should be the one to attend the hearing, not necessarily the personnel manager. All the personnel manager would have is file information—which is hearsay. If the claimant was discharged by the personnel manager for acts of which the supervisor has knowledge, then both the supervisor and the personnel manager should attend. At the hearing, the referee will always want to know what happened to cause the separation.

If the claimant was discharged for misconduct, be prepared to discuss:

1. The company rule the claimant violated.
2. Evidence that the claimant knew about the rule.
3. Disciplinary action taken when the rule was broken.
4. The events that occurred the last day of the claimant's employment.
5. What the claimant was told at the time of discharge.

As indicated elsewhere, all employees who had knowledge of the events leading to the discharge should appear as witnesses.

Subpoenas

If it is imperative that someone who no longer works for you appear as a witness, that person can be subpoenaed. Many employers never subpoena anyone because the word "subpoena" has a negative connotation. If this witness, who no longer works for you, is a "friendly" witness, that is, he or she will gladly testify for your company, you should still consider issuing a subpoena for the following reasons:

1. The subpoena, when given to the employer of the witness, will let the witness "off the hook." The new employer will not doubt the fact that he or she is going to an unemployment hearing.
2. Many states pay a subpoenaed witness. They don't pay much, but nevertheless, pay some remuneration.

If you know the witness will appear at the hearing, you can deliver the subpoena to the witness at the hearing. The local state unemployment office has the forms which you can request at the time of the hearing, or will tell you where they can be obtained.

Representation by an attorney

If you feel the case will be particularly difficult to win, or if the case has great repercussions, such as a multiclaimant hearing, you might want to consider representation by an attorney. However, before deciding to have representation by an attorney, we recommend you be sure it is necessary that the attorney attend. In most instances, you will need at least one witness from the company.

Miscellaneous suggestions

1. If the hearing is to take place in another city and you cannot arrange for a witness to attend, you can write the state and ask that

your testimony be taken locally, or wherever you so desire. This is not to say that you should make such a request if the hearing is only 10 or 20 miles away. However, if the hearing is in a place (whether within or outside of the state in which you are located) you cannot travel to, the request to have your testimony taken locally can and should be made.

2. At the hearing, don't be nervous; and treat the referee with respect, but don't be submissive. Bring out the facts you think will win the case.
3. Determine your rights at a hearing. Most referees will allow you to ask the claimant, or your witness, questions directed through the referee.

CAUTION. *Don't ask a question unless you know what the answer will be.* If you do, you'll probably be sorry you asked the question.

4. When you receive the referee's decision, if you won and the referee's original decision was reversed, a large credit to your account might be due, especially if the claimant has collected benefits for several months. Be sure you get the credit. The credit usually appears on a subsequent benefit charge statement.

Appeal board hearings

If you lose a referee hearing, you can again appeal and request that the appeal board, board of review, or review board in your state hear the case. In some states, they will meet as a board and hear witnesses. In other states, the employer (or claimant) submits the reasons why he or she thinks the referee's decision was erroneous, and there is no formal hearing.

Most employers do not pursue lost referee decisions to the appropriate review board. When they don't, they are not taking full advantage of the appeal process. Remember, a referee, even though guided by review board and circuit court cases, decides each hearing on what the referee believes to be the merits of the case. The referee could err just like anyone else. If you appeal to the appropriate review board, which has a formal hearing, be sure in your letter of appeal that you ask for a copy of the transcript from the referee's hearing so that you will know everything that was said. If the review board decides against you, the next alternative is to go to circuit court.

Summary of claims procedures

This, then, concludes our discussion of effective action an employer can take to control the handling of unemployment claims, determinations, and appeals. Exhibit 7–15 summarizes our discussion.

The person assigned to control the claims handling can become knowledgeable about all the matters discussed by reading, and/or a visit to a state unemployment agency. Once a few claims are protested and hearings attended, the person should have very few problems. If you are a particularly large employer in a state (or states), you might want to subscribe to services

EXHIBIT 7–15

Summary of claims procedure

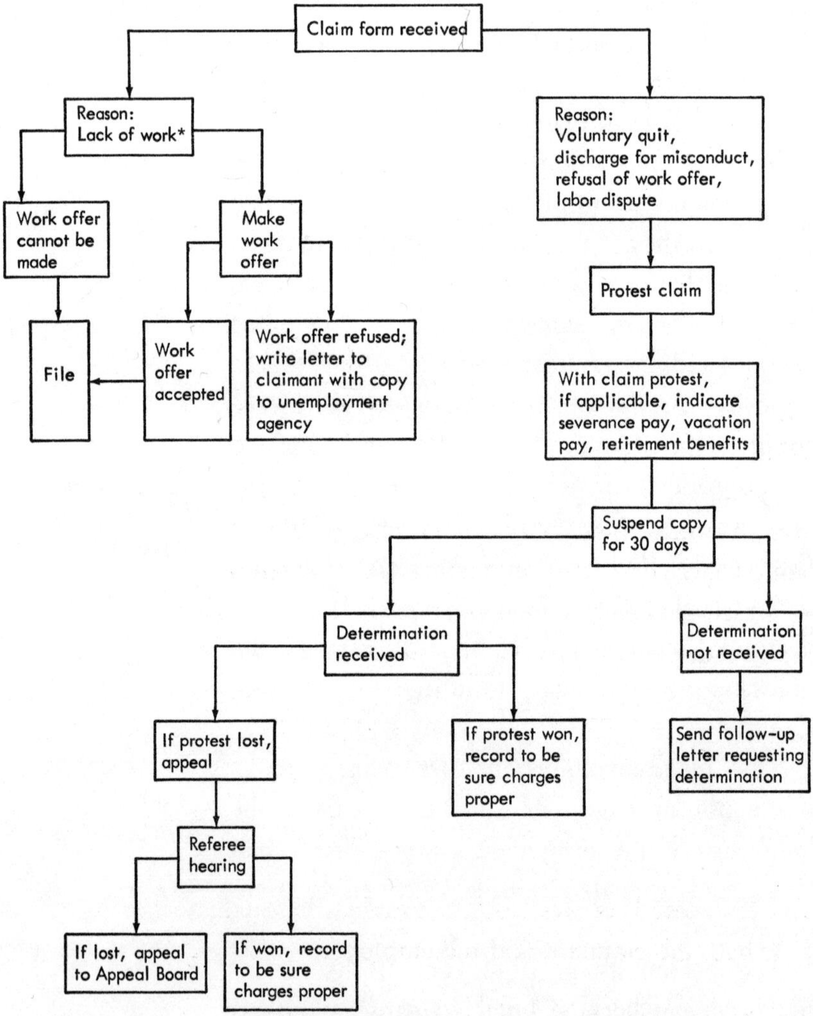

* If short-term layoff, indicate vacation pay and holiday pay received.

which give changes in the various regulations, such as Commerce Clearing House, 4025 W. Peterson Avenue, Chicago, Illinois, 60646. Prentice-Hall also provides a similar service.

chapter 8

Verification of benefit charges

Every state (except Texas[1]) and the District of Columbia issues a periodic charge statement indicating the amount of money you have been charged when a former employee has drawn unemployment benefits chargeable to you. See Exhibit 8–1 indicating the frequency at which charge statements are issued.

In order that you will have a better understanding of the various charge structures the states employ, following is a discussion of—

1. How the states determine which employers are "potentially" liable for the claimant's benefits, and
2. The resulting effect of a disqualification on both the claimant and the employer.

NOTE. Generally speaking, nonprofit institutions, and even municipalities and political subdivisions who are covered by the unemployment regulations, can apply the information contained in this chapter. The only exception is the

[1] In Texas a list of charges must be requested by the employer.

EXHIBIT 8–1

Frequency of charge statements

	Daily	*Weekly*	*Monthly*	*Quarterly*	*Semi-annually*	*Annually*
Alabama				X		
Alaska[a]						
Arizona				X		
Arkansas				X		
California						X
Colorado				X		
Connecticut						X
Delaware				X		
D.C.						X
Florida				X		
Georgia				X		
Hawaii				X		
Idaho						X
Illinois				X[b]		
Indiana			X			
Iowa				X		
Kansas						X
Kentucky				X		
Louisiana				X		
Maine			X			

EXHIBIT 8–1 (*continued*)

	Daily	*Weekly*	*Monthly*	*Quarterly*	*Semi-annually*	*Annually*
Maryland				X		
Massachusetts			X			
Michigan[c]	X			X		
Minnesota					X	
Mississippi				X		
Missouri				X		
Montana						X
Nebraska[c]	X			X		
Nevada						X
New Hampshire				X		
New Jersey		X				
New Mexico						X
New York		X				
North Carolina						X
North Dakota						X
Ohio			X			
Oklahoma	X					
Oregon			X			
Pennsylvania			X			
Rhode Island						X

EXHIBIT 8–1 (*concluded*)

	Daily	*Weekly*	*Monthly*	*Quarterly*	*Semi-annually*	*Annually*
South Carolina				X		
South Dakota			X			
Tennessee				X		
Texas[d]						
Utah[a]						
Vermont			X			
Virginia				X		
Washington[a]						
West Virginia			X			
Wisconsin[c]		X	X			
Wyoming						X

[a] Alaska: No charge to employers.
Utah: No charge to employers.
Washington: No charge to employers.

[b] Illinois: Charge statements issued three times per year covering the following periods of time:

1. July 1–September 30
2. October 1–March 31
3. April 1–June 30

[c] Michigan: Charges issued weekly and summarized quarterly.
Nebraska: Charges issued weekly and summarized quarterly.
Wisconsin: Charges issued weekly and summarized monthly.

[d] Texas: Charge statement issued upon request.

discussion about the effect of a disqualification on how employers are charged.

Chargeable employers

The states have various methods for identifying the employers who can be charged for benefits drawn by an unemployed worker. The methods of identifying potentially chargeable employers fall into four categories:

1. Prorated—charges are proportionate to base period earnings[2] with each employer. For example, suppose the claimant earned 40 percent of his or her total base period wages from employer A and 60 percent of his or her base period wages from employer B. Employer A, then, can be charged for 40 percent of the benefits given to the claimant and employer B can be charged for 60 percent of the benefits received by the claimant. See Exhibit 8–2 for the states that employ the prorated method of charging employers.
2. Inverse chronological order—charging is in inverse chronological order of employment in the base period. For example, suppose in the base period claimant worked for the following employers:

January 1–June 30	Employer A
July 1–July 10	Employer B
July 11–September 30	Employer C
October 1–December 31	Employer D

---

[2] As previously discussed, the base period of a claim is normally either the first 4 of the last 5 completed calendar quarters, or the 52 weeks prior to the filing of a claim, depending on the regulation in that state.

EXHIBIT 8–2
Potentially chargeable employers

There are four methods of charging employers for unemployment benefits.

Prorated: Charges are proportionate to base period earnings with each employer.

Inverse chronological order: Charging is in inverse chronological order of employment in the base period. The last employer in the base period is charged first, and so on, back to the first employer in the base period.

Benefit wage: All employers in the base period are charged an amount equal to the total wages earned (called benefit wages).

Last employer: Only the last employer (who meets certain conditions) is charged.

	Prorated	*Inverse chronological order*	*Benefit wage*	*Last employer*
Alabama			X[a]	
Alaska[b]				
Arizona	X			
Arkansas	X			
California	X			
Colorado		X		
Connecticut				X[c]
Delaware			X[a]	
Dist. of Col.	X			
Florida	X			

EXHIBIT 8–2 (*continued*)

	Prorated	*Inverse chronological order*	*Benefit wage*	*Last employer*
Georgia	X			
Hawaii	X			
Idaho[d]				
Illinois			X[a]	
Indiana		X		
Iowa		X		
Kansas	X			
Kentucky	X			
Louisiana	X			
Maine				X[e]
Maryland	X[f]			
Massachusetts		X		
Michigan		X		
Minnesota	X			
Mississippi	X			
Missouri		X		
Montana				X[g]
Nebraska		X		
Nevada	X			
New Hampshire				X[h]
New Jersey		X		

EXHIBIT 8–2 (*continued*)

	Prorated	*Inverse chronological order*	*Benefit wage*	*Last employer*
New Mexico	X			
New York		X		
North Carolina	X			
North Dakota	X			
Ohio		X		
Oklahoma			X[a]	
Oregon	X			
Pennsylvania	X			
Rhode Island		X		
South Carolina				X[i]
South Dakota		X		
Tennessee	X			
Texas	X			
Utah[j]				
Vermont				X[k]
Virginia			X[l]	
Washington[j]				
West Virginia				X[j]
Wisconsin		X		
Wyoming	X			

EXHIBIT 8–2 (*concluded*)

All employers in the base period charged after claimant draws:

[a] Alabama: Two full weeks of unemployment benefits.
Delaware: One full week of unemployment benefits.
Illinois: Three full weeks of unemployment benefits.
Oklahoma: Two full weeks of unemployment benefits.

[b] Alaska:
Utah:
Washington:
For these states, there are never any charges to an employer. The tax rates are determined on the variation in payroll—either from quarter to quarter, or year to year.

[c] Connecticut: Each employer who employed claimant in four or more different calendar weeks in preceeding 56-day period is charged.

[d] Idaho: Employer charged who paid greatest amount of wages to claimant in his base period.

[e] Maine: Benefits charged to most recent employer in base period for whom claimant worked at least five consecutive weeks is charged.

[f] Maryland: If at least 75 percent of base-period wages earned from one employer, then all benefits charged to this employer. If less than 75 percent of wages earned from one employer, charges prorated.

[g] New Hampshire: Benefits charged to the most recent employer in the base period for whom claimant worked at least five consecutive weeks.

[h] South Carolina: Benefits charged to the most recent employer in base period for whom claimant earned eight times his weekly benefit amount.

[i] Vermont: Benefits charged to most recent employer in base period for whom claimant earned at least $595.

[j] Virginia: The most recent employer in the base period for whom claimant worked 30 days (not necessarily consecutive) is charged *benefit wages*.

[k] West Virginia: Benefits charged to most recent employer in base period for whom claimant worked 30 days (not necessarily consecutive).

Note. See section on "Probationary Evaluation" at the beginning of Chapter 5. By knowing how employers can be charged, especially in the footnoted states above, a probationary period could be established that could possibly result in no benefit charges. For example, in Vermont, an employer could establish a probationary period so that all new employees are evaluated prior to earning $595. Chances are that if someone is separated prior to earning less than $595, another employer in the base period would have paid the claimant at least $595 and would be liable for his benefits. Applying this principle to the states mentioned, the following probationary period is recommended:

Maine: 4 consecutive weeks.
New Hampshire: 4 consecutive weeks.
South Carolina: 7 times minimum weekly benefit amount.
Vermont: Earnings less than $595.
Virginia: 29 days.
West Virginia: 29 days.

As explained above, charges would be in inverse chronological order. Employer D (the most recent employer) would be the first one charged; then, employers C, B, and A (in that order) would be charged. See Exhibit 8–2 for the states that employ the inverse chronological order method of charging employers.

3. Benefit wage—amount charged limited by benefit wages.[3] For example, suppose the claimant has the following benefit wage credits in his or her *base period:*

Employer A	$2,000
Employer B	1,000
Employer C	1,300

As soon as the claimant has drawn enough benefits so that employers will be charged, *all* employers in the base period will be charged an amount equal to the benefit wages earned by the claimant. In the above example, employer A will be charged $2,000, employer B will be charged $1,000, and employer C will be charged $1,300.

It is important to note that even though the claimant may draw just a few weeks of benefits, the employers in the base period will be charged the full benefit wages earned by that employee. The factor that springs

---

[3] Benefit wages are the actual wages earned during the base period converted to what is called "benefit wages." Thus, earnings of $2,000 in the base period would be converted to benefit wages of $2,000. Usually, there is a limit on the benefit wages for one claimant that can be charged to one employer.

the charge is the amount of benefits drawn. In Illinois, for example, when a claimant draws in unemployment benefits three times his or her weekly benefit amount (3 × WBA), all employers in the base period will be charged. If the above example was in Illinois, employers A, B, and C would be charged $2,000, $1,000, and $1,300, respectively, when the claimant would draw 3 × WBA. If the WBA was $60, all the claimant would have to draw would be (3 × $60) $180 for all of the charges to be triggered. See Exhibit 8–2 for the states that employ the benefit-wage method of charging employers.

4. Most recent employer—the last employer (prior to the filing of the claim that meets certain requirements) is the only liable employer. See Exhibit 8–2 for the states that employ the last employer method of charging employers.

After considering how states determine who are the potentially chargeable employers, let us now discuss the effect of a disqualification on both the claimant—and especially on the employer.

The so-called chargeable employers are potentially liable for unemployment benefits paid to claimants. However, the fact that an employer is potentially liable does not mean that employer will be charged. The word "potential" means exactly that! The state sets up the base period of the claim and determines the employers that could be charged for the claimant's unemployment benefits, in accordance with our discussion on "chargeable employers."

In some states, all employers that the claimant worked for in the base period, as well as the last employer, receive a claim notice at the time the claim is filed. In other states, only the claimant's last employer is notified. As we have discussed (and want to reemphasize), if you receive a claim notice and the claimant was separated from you for disqualifying reasons, that is, voluntary quit, discharge for misconduct, refusal of a work offer, and so on, the effect of your protest is, hopefully, a disqualification. The penalty imposed on the claimant when he or she is disqualified is usually one of the following, depending on the state involved:

1. A disqualification for a certain period of time; for example, three weeks.

or

2. A disqualification until the claimant works somewhere and earns wages; for example, until the claimant works and earns six times his or her weekly benefit amount.

Once the claimant has satisfied the requalification requirements, unemployment benefits can be collected, and usually the full amount.

You may be wondering, "if, after the requalification, the claimant can collect full benefits just as if there had been no disqualification, what good then does it to protest the claim?"

Relief of charges

The answer is: *By protesting the claim, you not only will delay the claimant's receipt of benefits (and he or she may have to find work),*

EXHIBIT 8-3
Benefit charges after disqualification

	Relief of charges[a] *(noncharging)*	*Duration suspension*[b]
Alabama	X	
Alaska		X
Arizona	X	
Arkansas	X	
California	X	
Colorado	X	
Connecticut	X	
Delaware	X	
District of Columbia		X
Florida	X	
Georgia	X	
Hawaii	X	
Idaho	X	
Illinois		X
Indiana		X
Iowa		X
Kansas	X	
Kentucky	X	
Louisiana		X
Maine	X	
Maryland		X
Massachusetts	X	
Michigan[c]		
Minnesota[c]	X	
Mississippi	X	
Missouri	X	
Montana	X	
Nebraska	X	
Nevada		X
New Hampshire	X	
New Jersey		X
New Mexico	X	
New York		X
North Carolina	X	
North Dakota		X
Ohio	X	
Oklahoma	X	
Oregon	X	
Pennsylvania	X	
Rhode Island	X	

EXHIBIT 8–3 (*continued*)

	Relief of charges[a] (*noncharging*)	*Duration suspension*[b]
South Carolina	X	
South Dakota	X	
Tennessee	X	
Texas	X	
Utah		X
Vermont	X	
Virginia	X	
Washington	X	
West Virginia	X	
Wisconsin	X	
Wyoming	X	

[a] *Relief of charges* (*noncharging*): On a normal disqualification for voluntary leaving, or discharge for misconduct, employer that obtained the disqualification is never to be charged.

[b] *Duration suspension:* After claimant serves the disqualification period, he can collect benefits chargeable to employer.

[c] *Michigan and Minnesota:* Combination of duration suspension and wage exclusion. Claimant can collect benefits chargeable to the employer after the disqualification period; however, the benefits for the disqualification period are subtracted from the total.

but in 38 states even though the claimant eventually draws the full 26 (*or whatever number*) *weeks of benefits, you should never be charged for these benefits.* This is called *relief of charges,* or *noncharging.* The claimant's benefits that normally would have been chargeable to you should come from state unemployment fund, not chargeable to any employer. Exhibit 8–3 indicates the states for which relief of charges can be obtained.

NOTE. As previously indicated, a nonprofit institution or political subdivision who elects to pay the state "dollar for dollar" (called "reimbursement") for benefits drawn by former employees cannot obtain relief of charges. This employer will have to reimburse the state for all benefits drawn and chargeable to him.

Of course, the state could err and charge you anyway. Therefore, a record of disqualifications received should be kept. When a charge statement is received, the employer must be sure *he was not charged anything.* If an error is found, an immediate protest letter should be sent to the state.

Duration suspension

In 11 states (see Exhibit 8–3), when a claimant is disqualified, unemployment benefits are *delayed* until the claimant serves several weeks of disqualification or goes back to work until a certain amount of wages is earned. In other words, after the claimant requalifies, he or she can still draw a full 26 weeks (or whatever) of benefits, and the employers are charged. Many employers feel that since the claimant may eventually draw benefits anyway, what's the use of protesting. Remember, by delaying the receipt of benefits, you will, in many instances, force the claimant to find work much quicker than if benefits would have been received immediately.

Duration suspension and wage exclusion

Wage exclusion means that the number of weeks a claimant is disqualified are subtracted from the claimant's total benefits. For example, suppose a claimant could have collected 26 weeks of benefits but is disqualified for 6 weeks because he or she voluntarily quit. Wage exclusion, in this instance, would result in the 6 weeks of benefits being subtracted from the total of 26 weeks. In other words, the claimant could only collect 20 weeks of benefits.

The combination of duration suspension and wage exclusion means the claimant's benefits will be delayed by the period of disqualification (6 weeks, in the above example) *and* the benefits for the disqualification period would also be subtracted from the total benefits the claimant could have received (26 weeks less 6 weeks in the above example). Another example is a claimant who would have drawn 15 weeks of unemployment and is disqualified for 6 weeks. The claimant could not collect any benefits for six weeks, and after the six weeks would collect nine weeks of unemployment compensation. See Exhibit 8–3. Michigan and Minnesota employ this method. A record could be maintained of people who are disqualified and the charges verified to be sure the benefits for the disqualification period are subtracted from the total.

Suggestion. If you have more than one location that could receive charge statements, controls should be established so that you, at least, verify charges in relief of charge states. Several alternatives follow—

1. Continue to allow the charge statements to be mailed from the state unemployment agency to the locations. However, obtain a copy of the charge statements from the locations—with appropriate notes indicating the reason for the charges.
2. Control the verification of charges from one location. Your other locations could send you copies of decisions disqualifying claimants, and the charge statements themselves

when received. Your office could then verify the charges.

3. Follow the same procedure as in (2) above; however, write to the state agencies and ask if the charge statements could be sent to you rather than to the other locations.

Additional notes

1. Pay particular attention to benefit charges after a change in corporate structure, including a merger or acquisition of *part* of a business. Perhaps part of a business was acquired (one location in a state, for example). Depending on the regulation in that state, if someone transferred to the new company files for unemployment, the charges should be prorated between the old and new employers. The regulation in that state should be checked.
2. With the advent of extended benefits and emergency extended benefits, extending benefits upwards to 65 weeks (and possibly longer), you should know how these benefits are going to be charged to employers. It is a simple matter to contact a state unemployment agency to determine the charge structure for extra benefits.
3. Keep a running record of the total amount of charges received so that the total amount of charges for the year that appears on your annual tax rate notice can be verified.
4. If you protest a charge and the state takes several months to issue a credit and your tax rate notice is issued with the charge still indicated, send a letter to the state protesting your rate notice.

chapter 9

Control procedures

An effective training program of personnel who will handle unemployment compensation matters must be established for maximum control. As we have emphasized, the control of these taxes, from the review and implementation of personnel policies to the training of supervisors, to the handling of claim forms, to verification of benefit charges and tax rates, to properly handling changes in corporate structure, cannot be haphazard! Management must realize that the control of unemployment compensation taxes is worthy of the time necessary to reduce this tax which, if unchecked, will cost needless thousands of dollars.

State tax payments

All matters concerned with tax rates should be controlled by the Tax department. Your unemployment tax rate is normally determined from the following factors:

1. Taxable payroll.
2. Quarterly contributions.
3. Benefit charges.

The taxable payroll and quarterly contribution figures are usually maintained in the tax department. If the personnel department verifies the benefit charges, they must keep the tax department informed of the total benefit charges; which should be verified with the charge figure on the rate notice.

Personnel policies

The personnel policies discussed should be considered in the light of already existing poli-

EXHIBIT 9–1

Supervisors' meeting

SUBJECTS TO BE DISCUSSED

I. Employer pays the cost of unemployment compensation
   A. Cost to the company the past year
II. Base period and benefit year—illustrate
III. Types of separations and result of disqualification
   A. Voluntary quit
   B. Discharge for misconduct
   C. Discharge for reasons other than misconduct
      1. Lack of work
      2. Unsatisfactory work
IV. Personnel policies
   A. Hiring procedures
      1. Selection
      2. Rules and handbooks
   B. Probationary evaluation
   C. Leaves of absence
   D. Absenteeism and tardiness
   E. Disciplinary action
   F. Termination procedures
      1. Voluntary quit
      2. Discharge
      3. Lack of work
      4. Completion of separation form
V. Proper disposition of unemployment claim forms and other data (if meeting of managers from various locations).

cies. Unemployment claims should be handled promptly and proper records kept. Supervisors' meetings should be held so that the supervisors (who normally implement the personnel policies) will be aware of their responsibilities in controlling unemployment compensation costs. See Exhibit 9–1 for a suggested format to use at a supervisors' meeting.

Once someone is charged with the overall responsibility of unemployment compensation cost control, thinks about control procedures, and obtains experience, the actual work and time involved can be held to a minimum.

The time and effort is worth it! Controlling this cost will not only save you money, but will provide benefits which transcend unemployment compensation, that is, improved personnel policies, improved tax policies, and the satisfaction of knowing your company has done its best to administer a program to reduce these costs.

Index